Mirror on the Wall
Am I like my mother after all...

By Viola Arriola

Published by BN Publishers

ISBN

978-1-956785-57-9

Dedications

To Lucy Bojorquez – my muse and historian, a long-time family friend.

To Nancy Twining – my confidant, my muse.

To my mother, Merced Yanez, who taught me to be strong, kind, forgiving, and true to myself; my muse throughout my book.

Last, but not least, thank you ladies for sharing the stories of your relationships with your mothers.

Contents

Introduction

My mother informed me at a very young age that I asked too many questions for a little girl and that I should be playing with my dolls or outside.

l was rather inquisitive during my childhood days. I was fortunate enough to become friends with little girls from different cultures. Along with the different cultures came the different foods, and all the children were bilingual. I was amazed at how the mothers were mostly raising their children alone, as the daddies were overseas or working. There was an Air Force base in Big Spring, Texas, the little town where I was born and raised, being my inquisitive self, I would ask my friends questions about their mom's accents, dress attire, and Kimonos, I ended up loving Japanese food and German food! I also admired all the mothers for their bravery and strength! They were like my mom, were stay-at-home mamas and good cooks!

I loved that we were like little sponges, recorders, and we respected our different cultures and found each lifestyle interesting and fun! We were so young and naive, adventurous and inquisitive I Our differences were like little surprises,

One summer hot day in 1955, my mother and I were waiting to board a bus to go visit relatives that lived in the same city. I was hot, thirsty, and pouty, and I wanted to get on the cool bus, I kept advancing in line and my mother kept pulling me back.

To my surprise, a lady and her little girl cut in front of us and the little girl proceeded to stare at me and told her mother, "Mama, look at the ugly little Meskin girl! Look at her dress and shoes!" The little girl was pretty, blue-eyed, and blonde-headed. Her dress was beautiful and shimmery with about a hundred petticoats it seemed. She reminded me of Nellie on "Little House on the Prairie!"

My dress was most likely a hand-me-down from my older sister who was five years older than I. The shoes were old and grungy looking and black. This ritual went on for a long time about letting all white people on the bus first, whether or not the weather was good or bad.

One day I told my sister about the little blonde girl and how mean she was to me, my sister asked me, "I wonder how she would feel if you were mean back?"

My sister then told me to turn to my mother and say, "Mama, look at that little nasty white girl, she's so ugly!"

The day came to be, and there was the little girl and her mother who never smiled and had a very flat affect, The little girl got in front of us, turned around, and was about to say something when I very loudly told my mom "Look at that nasty little white girl, she's ugly!"

The look of shock on my mother's face I shall never forget. The little girl's mother began to snort and mumble and they got on the bus. I was trying to beat them to get on first but my mother kept me back again!

Years later, I learned about a lady by the name of Rosa Louise McCauley Parks, who was an American activist during the civil rights movement and well known for her role in the Montgomery bus boycott on December 1, 1955. Rosa refused to sit in the rear section of the bus, which was the designated area for blacks and Hispanics, and all other non-white people. Rosa was arrested.

My mother and I never discussed my behavior that day when I spoke up for myself!

To this day, I wonder what happened to that little girl and her mother.

I learned that her mother was different from my mother, and the mothers of my friends. Later on, I realized that perhaps her mother was behaving the way she thought she was supposed to and my mother was too!

I didn't feel good after I said what I did to the little girl, and I still wish to this day that I had been able to apologize or smile sweetly at her.

Much later, my sister and I were talking about my bus incident and I told her. "I could have gone to jail at almost five years old!"

My sister responded, "I would have taken you snacks!"

My book is about daughter/mother relationships, some happy ones, some sad ones. All empowering! Some daughters kept their traditions alive, while others made new ones! You may read some stories that you may relate to. All are meant to empower and inspire you in some way!

Viola Arriola

2023

My mission in life is not merely to survive, but to thrive, and to do so with some passion, some compassion, some humor, and some style.

– Maya Angelou

There is no greater agony than bearing an untold story inside you.

– Maya Angelou

When we face the things we're ashamed of or the things we think others will judge us for, then we find peace.

– Sue Fitzmaurice

You may not control all the events that happen to you, but you can decide not to be reduced by them.

– Maya Angelou

Create the highest grandest vision possible for your life, because you become what you believe.

– Oprah Winfrey

Friends commented on my relationship with my mother and asked if we had always had a close relationship. Actually, it was not until after I married that mom and I became closer. Mom made sure I knew she was not my friend, nor did she want to be! Mom was my mother and I was her daughter. After having shared this bit of information with my friends, they, in turn, shared their stories with me! My friends and women who contributed their stories and my mom, my muse, inspired my story, and book.

Some stories are happy, others are sad. Some have never been told before. Several ladies thanked me because, at last, they had their closure...

My Own Insight

Give yourself a gift of your own Insight. – Hallmark movie (said in the movie)

Being a social worker for over thirty years, I have always given of myself to others.

I have to admit that sometimes, I was ok, but most of the time, have been drained afterward. If I needed time for myself or required any soul-searching moments, there was never enough time! Now I've realized that I just never have made time for myself, and also, that I don't practice what I preach.

After hearing this character in a movie suggest this to another character, it finally hit me! I do have gifts; I share these gifts with others and I definitely need to save little boxes of my own insight for my own personal emergencies!

I have a feeling I'm going to need to open up these little parcels often. I've heard that some people think social workers and psychologists are "different." Well, guess what folks? You're right. I've always known that I hear the beat of a different drummer, and that has always been fine with me.

Fashion

My mother was a lot like me, or rather, I was so much like her in this aspect. She didn't care that she dressed differently than the other mothers. Mom wore pants every day unless she was going to church, a funeral, or a wedding. My mom was a Hispanic "June Cleaver" in pants! She even wore a pantsuit on her wedding day!

My mother's morning ritual was drawing the curtains to let in the sunshine of the day. A ritual passed down to me....

My Daughters

A pinch of this and a spoonful of that and fair to partly cloudy... with a chance of jalapenos!

Laura Collins

Pharmacy tech, stay-at-home wife, firstborn, daring, and caring. She started walking at nine months, and actually learned to run before walking – and never stopped talking!

– A Cute Story –

Laura loved to buy things for her grandmother (my mom). We were at the department store and looking at underwear, when out of her five-year-old mouth came, "Please buy grandmother panties! She uses safety pins to keep them up! All I could think of was, "Ouch!" Needless to say, I bought the panties...

Another time, I was reading the newspaper and there was a picture of her and a few other students holding a certificate for eating all of their vegetables for a month! When she got home from school, I confronted her and her response was, "I ate a double portion of the ones I did eat!" Tomatoes and carrots and peas, oh my,..

Pamela Martinez

Educational Diagnostician, the second born, sincere and outspoken. She learned to walk when she got too heavy to be carried at a year old.

- A Scary Baby Story –

After Pamela decided to walk, she enjoyed walking away from us, and we would run after her. It became a fun game for her! She would giggle and say, "More!"

In December when she was a year and three months old, I took her with me to the mall. There was Christmas music playing and bells ringing. She was in her baby stroller.

Her daddy Gilbert and I had made sure that Pamela had bells on her shoes so we could hear her when she was on the move!

I turned around to look at a blouse, still holding onto her stroller and rolling it back and forth because she was being fussy. I turned down to look at her and she was gone! I panicked and screamed and security and police were asking me questions. Five minutes had gone by when I heard a tiny familiar voice say, "Hi Mama!" Oh, and she had a big balloon tied around her wrist I stopped shopping and we went home. Lesson learned and I took a nap with her in her crib!

- To my daughters –

In the journal of my heart, I wouldn't change a thing about y'all...

Seasonings of My Life

My grandchildren are like spices to my heart!

Jarrett – The Oregano

Bold, but if truth be told, has a heart of pure gold

Macy – The Rosemary

Her light shines bright through all kinds of weather.

She refuses to lose sight.

Always keeping it together.

Lindsey – The Paprika

The colorful touch to boring dishes.

She's dramatic, sometimes calm, like a beautiful dove.

Don't allow her to fool you, inside she's pure love.

Emily – The Cinnamon

Personality plus, kind yet fierce.

Adding sweet spice to life.

Ethan – The Salsa

A mixture of all of the above.

Talent and looks will surely go down in the books, and his goals and dreams are not forsaken.

May he be blessed in abundance for the path he has taken.

Native American Women

According to Indians.org, women played a very important role in the life of Native Americans. They were wives and mothers, helped the men with hunting buffalo, harvested them, skinned the buffalo, cut them, and prepared the meals! The women were also the builders of the homes, warriors, fanners, and were excellent at making clothes and jewelry. The men treated the women with respect and realized they were strong and brought consistency to their lives.

Recently, I found out I am 49% Native American. My great-grandmother on my mother's side was Sioux, and my great-grandmother on my father's side was Mescalero.

Monday-Sunday Undies

Mom taught my sisters Sulema, Adelinda, and me to take care of our bodies, skin, and appearance. "Make sure your clothes are clean and not wrinkled and please do not forget to have clean underwear on!" Mom told us that it would be terrible to be in an accident, be taken to the hospital, and be wearing torn or soiled underwear!

Of course, I was terrified! In the fifth grade, Mom bought my sister and me panties with the days of the week embroidered on each panty. I am not sure what happened but it was Friday and I could not find the underwear for that day, so I opted for the Saturday one. I was scared to death that I would fall or break a leg, be transported to the hospital, and they would see that I was not wearing the panty of the day!

I got through the day without incident, ran home, and told Mom about my horrible panty day and I remember her laughing so hard the tears ran down her cheeks! That is when she explained that as long as they were not torn and soiled, that was all that mattered! Whew! What a relief that was and I vowed to not ever buy panties embroidered with days if I ever had girls!

I shared this story with my husband Meliton and a few weeks later, I received panties with the day of the week on them! They still make them in big girl sizes! I still wear the wrong day panties!

Hanging by Her Underwear and the Sticker Patch

My sister Sulema and I loved to sneak out of our bedroom window to hide in the alley and listen to a local band that used to practice directly behind our house. One summer night we decided we would sneak out and listen to the band. I was wearing a nightgown and my sister had on her baby doll pajamas.

I proceed to jump out of the window and step into a sticker patch! I scream and scare my sister as she is trying to get out of the window by her underwear and pajamas that are stuck on a nail! The light suddenly comes on and my daddy pulls my sister back inside the room and yells at me to go around to the kitchen door! I get to the door, and I'm pulling the stickers out of my feet and my dad is standing by the door with the meanest look that I have ever seen on his face!

He points to our room and I comply and crawl into my bed, my feet bloody and in pain and my sister is giggling under the sheets! Then she turns on the flashlight and proceeds to show me her torn pajamas and underwear! We both lost it and began to laugh and here comes my dad again!

Eyes Behind Her Head

Mama was smart, wise, and perceptive. My siblings and I just knew she had eyes in the back of her head! I remember asking her once how she knew when we were in trouble, sad, or keeping things from her. Mama responded, "Silly girl, I was your age once! I had the same feelings, thoughts, and notions just like you."

The Ring (Mom tattles on me)

One day I decided to go buy myself a ring. I didn't have a lot of rings then. I walked into the jewelry store, and picked out the ring I wanted, only to learn that it was way beyond what I could afford! So, what do I do? I placed it on layaway! I was so excited and scared just a little, that I had a secret and did not want my hubby Gilbert to find out! I'm feeling kind of guilty and am dying to share my secret with someone. I receive a phone call from Mama inviting me to dinner, so I say to myself, "Aha, here's my chance to share my secret with someone else!" I mean, who better than my mother, right?

So, I announce as I enter Mama's kitchen.

"Mama, guess what I did today?" She quickly asks, "What?"

I proudly announce "I just placed a ring on layaway!"

Mama responded, "Really? What does it look like?" So, I proceeded to describe my ring to her, and Mama said in Spanish, "Que bonito!" (English translation, "How pretty!") I mentioned to Mama not to tell my hubby, and she said she wouldn't. About thirty minutes later, my hubby walked in the door and Mama exclaimed, "You wouldn't believe what your wife did!" I had a mouthful of food and began to choke on my food! My secret was out and was not even two hours old. Later I asked Mama why she had done this, and she responded, "I just wanted to see your facial expression!" I answered, "I almost choked on my food!" Mama then said, "Oh, I'm sorry Mija!" There were other secrets that I shared with her and she kept them under her hat, I think.

Keep Some Secrets for Yourself

My mom told me to not tell all my secrets to anyone, to save some for myself!

Especially to men, because they can turn it around and use it against you! Mom said to be careful with friends too, as some couldn't keep their own secrets much less someone else's! Good advice Mom!

The Unfortunate Red Hen

My mother's mom, Grandma Lala, had a comadre/friend that would travel for miles over the mountains of Shafter, TX. This comadre would carry a burlap sack with several chickens in it. She would walk to Shafter and barter with other folks who also had food, fruit, vegetables, beans, etc.

The comadre would stop by Grandma Lala's house to rest and have dinner and would stay overnight. Apparently, it was customary to bring a small gift to your hostess, especially if you were getting fed and spending the night. Other friends would bring a small token of appreciation.

The comadre had good intentions as she would explain to Grandma Lala that she had a beautiful red hen for her but while she was crossing the river, it got away and drowned! This was the excuse every two weeks when the comadre would come into town on her business ventures.

Aunts and uncles would ask Grandma, "Why don't you tell her you will take another chicken?"

To which my aunts would ask, "Why is it always your red hen that drowns?!" The laughter was endless every time.

Chicken Brain Freeze at Rancho Sueno Dorado

My friends Lucy and Albert have chickens that love ice cream! Albert will sit in the shade and the chickens get in line for a taste of ice cream. They're not picky either! Some chickens go around hiccupping for a while!

Chickens with Dementia

One morning I was going to Lucy and Albert's house for breakfast from their small cabin that they call "Motel 6." I opened the screen door, looked down and there was a blue egg right in front of my feet! I picked it up and set it by the side of the cabin.

As I continued on my way to the house for breakfast, I noticed another colored egg inside the dog house! I get to the house and I immediately tell Lucy and Albert about the colored eggs and asked if anyone was playing tricks on me?

Albert said, "We have a crazy chicken that lays them wherever she wants to!" My cousin Barbara from California was visiting with them also and added, "Chicken butts become old and after a while, their eggs just roll out!"

We all busted out laughing and I choked on my toast! Albert said that he thought the chickens lay colored eggs because of the feed. It had been my first visit with Albert and Lucy, and I had wished I had been invisible when that came out of my cousin's mouth!

According to Life Insider

By Staff Contributor

February 21, 2020

Talks about how even though most people do not realize it, some of the most important and strongest people in our lives are our mothers!

The author claims that our mothers are not given the recognition they deserve.

The author states that our mothers shape us into the best version of ourselves and prepare us for the real world.

I personally agree with the author. Having a strong mother did make me strong!

Welcome Home

By Viola Arriolas

She had a smile on her face that day. Her fears were gone, her heart felt light. She felt the warmth; the sun was bright. She had a smile on her face that day. Her soul felt joy, and her mind was clear. She had a smile on her face that day,

Her spirit was free, she found her voice, and deep inside she made her choice. She had a smile on her face that day.

With all her strength, with all her might, she knew that she would be alright. She had a smile on her face that day.

She would enjoy her God-given gifts, her todays and her tomorrows, the sun and moonlight, and the peace within.

When a mother dies, a daughter's mourning never completely ends.

– Hope Edelman, author

Mother's Day

Happy Mother's Day to all the Mamas of the world!

Spirit of Mama

By Viola Arriola

A voice soft as raindrops on a warm summer day

Eyes that smile and twinkle like stars far away

A heart full of love and forgiveness like the first day of spring

Hands so soft like an angel wing

Memories like pictures are Imprints that keep playing in my head

They hum and dance before me when I am feeling sad

At times I do invite them back so I can be the host

They will return to comfort me when I need them the most!

Being a mother is learning about strengths you didn't know you had. ... And dealing with fears that you didn't know existed.

- Linda Wooten

Mirror on the Wall...

My daughter Pam called me to let me know her husband Tracy had informed her that she screams and acts like her mom (me) when he is driving! I tend to get a bit paranoid if I'm not driving,

A few days later, my daughter called me again. This time to let me know she had to get eyeglasses, and when she looked at her-self in the mirror, she saw me! I'm not sure if she wants to see me every time, she sees herself, but she did say "Mirror mirror, on the wall, I look like my mother after all!"

Pay Attention to Your Body

A few years ago, I just was not feeling like myself. My back began to hurt on the right side and I ignored it as it would come and go. In my mind, I would tell myself, "Quit ignoring this and see a doctor!" I finally began paying attention to what my body was trying to tell me, and sure enough, I had kidney cancer, but it was on my left kidney.

My kidney was removed and the doctor asked if I had an inner voice telling me to get myself checked and I told him that my head, body, and soul were alerting me!

According to my surgeon, I went in just in time and the cancer did not spread. I have one kidney that is smaller but it does work. I call him "The Kid!" I am blessed! Pay close attention to your body and mind.

Purple Lipstick, Orange Nails and Toes, Oh My!

The night before my kidney biopsy, I took a long bath, and I did my hair, nails, and toes. The morning of my biopsy, I made sure my makeup looked good, and I wore my darkest purple lipstick! My sweatshirt and pants had to match and so did my socks and ten-nis shoes. I have this OCD-ness about your nails and toes looking nice and colorful. To this day, I tell my daughters and grand-daughters to make sure these parts of their bodies look good!

Before I was wheeled in for my procedure, I asked my daughter if my purple lipstick was still on my lips ok. To my dis-may, she said, "Mom, it's not purple!" My daughter is still disagreeing with me about my purple lipstick! I know it was purple and I knew about the color purple way before she did! Eww!

THE STORIES

Viola-My Story, Part I

I am the second born of six siblings, three girls and three boys. My sister Sulema (Sue) was five years older than me, and then my brothers Sonny, Arthur, Roland, and my little sister Adelinda were two years apart.

My sister Sue wasn't used to having a baby sister in the house and proceeded to prove it the first couple of weeks of my birth! She overheard my mother talking on the phone about how tiny I was and that I could possibly fit in a shoebox. I was a full-term baby but I had a low birth weight due to my mother smoking the whole nine months while she was pregnant with me.

"Enter me, at four pounds."

My mother was not told not to smoke while she was pregnant. The doctors even smoked while seeing patients back then!

The doctor told my mother to take me home and carry me on a pillow and that hopefully, I would "thrive!"

One day when my mom was out hanging up clothes, my sister found a shoebox and paraded me around the house!

My mother had no family in town to assist her with chores around the house and cooking. She didn't have time to relax and take it slow after giving birth. My mother continued to wash by hand, hang clothes out on the line and prepare meals for my father who did not know how to even boil water!

Meanwhile, my sister was hard at work planning her next adventure with tiny me.

Sue had once again overheard my mother telling a comadre that I did not have much of a nose and she did not know how I could breathe. My sister was found with scissors in my nostrils, and was in the process of opening them up!

My mother calmly told her to move her hand and she stepped and gently removed the scissors from my tiny nose. My mom asked Sue why she had done such a thing, and she replied, "I was helping her to breathe!"

My grandmother had died from cancer at a young age when Mom was sixteen.

Mother had pretty much raised her younger brothers and sisters from the age of six.

Her mother, my grandmother who I had never met, had made my mother promise her that the family would remain close after she was gone, and mother kept her promise!

When my brother was born, I became very jealous, would not eat, pulled my hair out, and pinched and pulled my baby brother's hair!

My parents worried about me and my baby brother and sent me to stay with an aunt and uncle who had two boys and so I got a lot of attention! After a few months, my mother told my aunt to bring me back home and I did not want to go! I was forced to go home. Mom said I was nicer to my brother Sonny.

My other siblings were okay with each other and there were no other jealousy incidents!

My mother was a stay-at-home mom and we loved it! Some of the mothers of my friends worked and our friends were welcomed into our home to enjoy a meal or two with us, my mother would often ask my father how there was always enough for the eight of us plus one or two extras.

My sister Sue was at it again, and could not understand why I always fought for the wings of the chicken, and decided she wanted them, so I got the chicken leg. Later on, while we were growing up, Mother would prepare two chickens. Then Sue decided she missed the leg after all!

My dad began to get worse health-wise and eventually required dialysis for his kidney failure. Mom stayed with him through his hospitalizations, and I would stay with him when I could.

I married and had two girls and my mother helped me with them and they loved being at her house. I began to attend college and was involved in organizations and was even on the school board. Mother was not on board with me having extracurricular activities outside the home. She could not understand why I wanted to get educated.

Mom had female friends that would go see her and have coffee and pastries. She helped in church activities until she no longer could and was known for her strong coffee. My sister would say a spoon can stand up in her coffee cup!

Later on, through the years, she told me how proud she was of me for doing every-thing I was doing and for my accomplishments and those of my sisters also.

Dad passed away and Mom really went down. She had been his caregiver for so many years. Several years later, Mom be-came ill with COPD and passed away. She and I were very close and my daughter Laura took care of Mom while she was ill.

Mom had taught me to be strong, loving, and nurturing and was proud of me and all her children!

I have two daughters, Laura and Pamela.

They are both very loving and caring and have children of their own. Like my mother and I, their family comes first. I have shared my spirituality with them and now it's up to them to live their lives to the fullest with love in their hearts. I pray that my daughters teach my granddaughters Macy and Lindsey to be true to themselves, as well as how to be loving, caring, and forgiving. I pray that they may also pass these gifts to their daughters, Paisley and Kenna.

Viola-My Story, Part II

Every day Mom made fresh tortillas, meat, and beans. She swore her children would have some form of meat every day because while she was growing up, they only had meat on Sundays and holidays. We all have high cholesterol! Mother was a fantastic cook and she could put together a delicious meal in no time.

If my brothers wanted seconds or thirds, they would call my name and open their mouths so I could see the food they were chewing. I, of course, would scream and gag and leave the table, and Mom would get on to the boys.

Besides cooking and cleaning and taking care of all our needs, my mother took care of my dad's diet as he had renal failure and had to be on a strict diet. My dad was also in the hospital a lot and Mom stayed with him in the hospital and my sister and I took care of the house and younger siblings.

Mother had a special relationship with each of us. She later told us that she knew each of us in and out and our different personalities. She loved us all the same but in her motherly love and intuition knew exactly what each of us needed!

Our holidays were awesome! Christmas was celebrated on Christmas Eve. Mother would prepare tamales - homemade – and leave them cooking while we would attend Midnight Mass. Afterward, we would eat, and open gifts. Other holidays were just as much fun with wonderful food and being surrounded by family and friends,

I loved the way Mom would see that we were all looked after and even though she didn't tell us she loved us every day, she did say it for our birthdays, when we were sick, and we knew, we understood. We were all affectionate with Mom, kissing her and hugging her. We spoiled her!

My mother was strict with us girls, and not so much with the boys. I asked her why and she said boys were boys and girls had a lot more to lose.

My mom knew I did not approve and through the years attempted to try and make me understand her rationale! My mother did give my sisters and me advice about relationships, growing up and the importance of taking care of ourselves, and our bodies, and about being respectful to others and ourselves. She told me that a lady must not go around showing her breasts, etc. My mom said, "A lady must remain a mystery!" All I could envision was guys going around with a magnifying glass, like Sherlock Holmes, looking me over!

When I was fifteen years old, I had made a date with three different guys, not knowing they would all show up at the same time, and they did! I was washing dishes, when out of the window, there they were in their cars, I begged Mom to tell them I was not home, but instead, she grabbed me by the arm and shoved me out the door! Need-less to say, that did not go very well. My mom kept a clean house and even though it was small, it was tidy and cute!

On the weekends, the girls would make their own beds and the brothers' beds as well. I was the designated dishwasher after my sister went off to college. I attempted to "pull the wool over my mom's eyes" and I would hide the greasy pans because I did not want to wash them and then I was in trouble!

I did not have my mother's love of cooking or cleaning the house, but we did share our love for music, dancing, shoes, perfume, and jewelry. I love to cook now and managed to get recipes over the phone, or by watching. Mom did not measure any-thing, she just used a pinch of this and that!

A few weeks before Mom passed away, I was looking at her as she sat smoking her cigarette still! She motioned me over, grabbed my hand, and kissed it. She also winked at me. That was her way of saying she loved me and she was going to be ok and so was I! I still participate in my Mother's daily routine of opening the curtains/blinds to let the sunshine and blessings in and start the day!

In the end, we'll all become stories.

- Margaret Atwood

Alma

Alma is the youngest of four siblings. She said she was the baby and only girl, and has three older brothers. Alma and her mother get along well, and she stated "We're super close." According to Alma they talk on the phone at least three times a day.

She described the many things she loves about her mom and how she admires how generous her mother is with others.

Alma added that she also loves her mother's sense of humor and how her mom's nieces look up to her and call to talk about "stuff." Alma likes that her mother is non-judgmental and is very open-minded. "Holidays were always fun!" Alma remembers how Thanksgiving was spent at her grandmother's house. She said her mom would cook and they would load everything up and go to the grandmother's and aunt's home.

Alma described Christmas as being delightful! She said they would attend midnight mass and open up gifts. Alma remembers how grateful she and siblings were for the gifts they received. Her mother taught her how to make biscochos (Mexican wedding cookies) and how to cook. Alma would help her mom bake, and her father and her would distribute pound cakes to aunts and uncles for Christmas.

Alma stated she loved the feeling of giving and that definitely the gift of giving was the biggest lesson she learned from her mom!

When Alma was a teenager, she did not like her mom because of the rules that were in place for her, but not for her brothers.

Alma did not understand her mother's rationale, but stated that once she became an adult, her thought process changed and she loves their closeness and awesome relationship.

Alma added that she hated to think of the day she will no longer be able to call her mother to hear something funny or stupid!

Grace

Grace is the 2nd of 5 siblings. When she was five years old, her mother left her at her step father's home. He brought her up and raised her the best he could. Grace said her step dad was married, and the wife was emotionally, verbally and physically abusive to her. She was told not to say anything to her step dad.

At age 14, Grace ran away to look for her biological mother. She did locate her mother who was living with Grace's grand-mother. There was no connection of love or interest in her mother toward Grace, but she remained living with her mother and grandmother. She was neglected and lonely. Grace's mother would come and go and left the siblings with her grandmother. Grace stated she became pregnant when she was in junior high. She lived on her own and worked to support herself and her baby.

Grace obtained a vocation and is happy with her job. She has no contact with her mother or siblings. She said she is happier this way. Grace has one daughter and is a grandmother. She is teaching her daughter to be strong and independent.

Kimberly

Kimberly was the only child and was close to both her mom and dad. While her father worked, Kimberly's mom was patient and loving with her. She considered her mom her best friend. Kimberly said her mom taught her how to have fun, be a friend, and how to be loving and kind.

She shared the love of Country music with her mother and father and fondly remembers them buying her a country music cassette tape by the group Alabama and being "hooked" on country music since then.

Kimberly enjoyed having slumber parties, skipping school, and going to do fun things with her mom when she didn't go to school!

Kimberly's mother supported her all through school and college. Kimberly's mother was proud that she wanted to be a social worker.

Her mother told her that she was not feeling well after Kimberly had given her a birthday party. A year later she passed away from cancer. Her father died in a truck wreck 4 years later. Kimberly said she is grateful for her mother having taught her to be the person she is today.

Kimberly has no daughters. She has one son that she loves and supports him as he was diagnosed with Asperger's and is now living in a group home. Kimberly visits him twice a month and makes sure she shares her love and affection with him.

Maria Juanita

Maria Juanita is the 6th child of 7 siblings. She grew up in a small Texas town. Ac-cording to Maria Juanita her mother was strict, but very loving. Maria Juanita said her mother was so strict that she couldn't go across the street without asking permission. She said she had a happy childhood.

Maria Juanita explained how her three oldest siblings were grown up and living on their own. One of those siblings was a female, and Maria Juanita described growing up without the "sister experience".

Holidays were happy and fun filled. Her mother and grandmother would prepare tamales and tortillas from scratch. Christ-mas became very difficult for the family as her grandmother died on Christmas Day. According to Maria Juanita her mother in-stilled in her the love for Jesus and Mary.

She explained that she realizes now why her mother was so protective of her.

Adel

Adel is the 3rd of 7 siblings. Her mother was a single mom. She remembers growing up poor and not having her mother around much as she worked hard and long hours to make sure they had food and clothes. Her mother was not affectionate, but Adel and her siblings knew and felt that they were loved. It was just understood. She explained that as she and her siblings grew older, the mother was affectionate and loving.

Adel said they did not celebrate the holidays due to her mother having to work, but she does recall one year when her mother brought a Christmas tree home. Adel said someone had given it to them.

Her mother would give them a paper sack with candy and fruit, and how her gesture was very much appreciated! Adel stated how she admired her mother for being strong, but didn't like that she was tired all the time from working so hard,

Adel is grateful to her mother for teaching her how to cook and keep a clean and tidy home. She said she loved her mother and her mother loved her.

Jes

Jes is the second of 2 siblings. She described growing up as fun, but lonely as she got older. Jes said she was not close to her mom as a teen but they became close during her adulthood. They did not get along during Jes's teen years.

She described holidays as happy and fun. Jes appreciates how her mother taught her how to be kind towards others. "Mother always tried to make us smile when we were mad or sad!" Jess didn't like it when she felt that her mother seemed to choose work more important than family. Jes tries to balance work and family the best she can and is close to her children.

She has one "beautiful smart daughter." Jes has taught her to "love others and treat them the way you want to be treated, be strong, Independent, Love Jesus and stand your ground."

Evette

Evette is the second of 3 siblings. She recalls how kind, gentle, loving and caring her mother was. Evette lost her mother recently. She said she got along well with her mother, and described how warm, loving and fun holidays were.

Evette stated she loved how her mother was so nurturing. "There was nothing about her that I disliked!" According to Evette she learned many things from her mother. Evette learned how to cook, sew, keep house, and how to live a good life.

Evette has one daughter and they get along well. "I have taught her how to care and love her family, cook and many other things that my mother taught me!"

Dina

Dina is the second of four siblings. She stated she got along with her mom. "Holidays were fun and everyone came to my parents' home until my parents passed away."

Dina said there was plenty of food and fun during the holidays. According to Dina, her mother was soft spoken and took care of Dina and her siblings,

Dina explained that her mother "held the wrong things to be important." Her mother felt you needed to be married, pretty and have money. Dina explained "I didn't qualify! I was the least attractive girl in my family. That being said, mother was a fine Christian with flaws like the rest of us." She informed how her mother was partial to her only brother, and her sisters were ranked by their looks and money. Dina said "I was always number 4."

Dina is grateful to her mother for teaching her how to cook and look after others. She said her mother was a peacemaker, and handed the title to Dina.

Dina's mother passed away recently and is truly missed by Dina and the family.

Maria Pilar

Maria Pilar is the youngest of 11 siblings.

She has 5 sisters and 3 brothers living.

Maria Pilar describes her childhood as loving, fun, and she always had attention from all her older siblings. She was spoiled by them all, being the baby of the family.

Marla Pilar stated that she had a special bond with her mother and will forever treasure that special bond. First, she was born on her mother's birthday. Secondly, her mother had her when she was 39 (menopausal baby). Her older brothers and sisters helped with the smaller children. Her oldest brother was 16, and oldest sister was 15, when she was born.

Maria Pilar stated that holidays were happy and fun. "We would all gather with the family. Our grown adult siblings would join us with their spouses. We would get so excited because they would also bring us presents. My adult sister, who was already married, learned how to make tamales so we started that tradition for several years.

We would attend midnight mass on Christ-mas Eve."

Maria Pilar stated that her mother was a stay-at-home mom. Her father always worked hard to provide for the family. She remembers coming home from school to the smell of freshly made tortillas aroming the house. That was always a very heartwarming smell to her. She states her mother was very kind, and caring. She states her mother was her everything. She remembers not liking school because she al-ways wanted to stay home with her mother instead. The best thing she loved about her mom was her serene spirit.

Marla Pilar stated her mother and father would take care of her children while she and her husband worked. Her children also had a special bond with her mother. Her mother passed away at the age of 80, when Maria Pilar was 41. Her children were able to care for both of her parents in their elderly age. Which makes Marla Pilar very proud and happy.

Maria Pilar has one daughter and one son. She has a very good relationship with both of her children. Her daughter is not married. She has a very close bond with her daughter. They get along very well and spend a lot of time with each other. She hopes that she has taught her daughter to be a good loving wife to her future husband, and children.

She has a close bond with her son. "As a married son, our relationship has changed into more of ensuring that I am ok." Her son is married and has 3 girls and one boy. She has a very special bond with her grandchildren. She has written 2 books that she has dedicated to 2 of her granddaughters. She plans on writing more books to dedicate to the rest of her grandchildren. She states her grandchildren are her inspiration, and hopes to instill love, caring and kindness to them.

Lucy

Lucy was the fourth born of nine siblings and was the oldest of the girls. There were six girls and three boys. There is only one sibling and Lucy left.

Lucy was born in Marfa, Texas, but her father moved the family to Shafter, Texas, a mining community. Lucy's mother was unaffectionate. Luckily, she was close to her father who was very affectionate and was a good father to his children. Her mother kept the home spotless and was all about discipline according to Lucy.

It was then that Lucy said she vowed to be loving and not cold to her children if she ever had any!

Everyone in the family had their own chores to be done.

Lucy was growing up quickly and her mother did not have "the mother/daughter talk." Lucy explained that her father had the father/daughter talk with her. She said "that's how I learned about 'the birds and the bees!'"

Lucy laughed and said her mother was too busy raising nine children and keeping house that she had not had the time to be a loving mother. Lucy said her mother did not like Lucy's father, but she had refused to go into detail about it. Lucy's dad was eventually hit by a car while walking and passed away.

Eventually, Lucy moved to California and began dating a young man. They dated for a while and then one day she met Albert. Albert was the one for her and she said her previous boyfriend had to go!

Lucy and Albert eloped and her father forgave her and her mother told Lucy she did not like Albert. She told Lucy "Albert is worth about as much as his weight!" He was a short thin man. In time, Lucy's mother grew to like Albert.

Albert had been born and raised in California and had no intention of leaving.

Lucy, however, had dreams of returning home to Shafter and convinced Albert to move back to Shafter. They worked hard on their little ranch, and they built a home on their land on top of a mountain. They called their ranch "Sueno Dorado" or Golden Dream.

Lucy became an LVN nurse and Albert worked in the fields and repaired machinery. They had two sons that were born in Shafter and grew up and graduated and went off to college, married, and had children.

Lucy did raise and was involved in their lives, nieces, and other female children and they have remained close through the years.

Lucy liked to dress nice, as did her mother. She enjoyed fixing her hair in the latest styles. Lucy is a great cook just like her mother was. She prepares delicious meals and has kept tradition and made a few of her own along the way!

Lucy's mother taught her that men were supposed to be served first for all meals, holidays, and when the men returned home from a hard day's work. Lucy spoiled Albert and waited on him hand and foot! He eventually retired and Lucy retired also.

Lucy's mother also catered to her husband and sons. The Hispanic tradition to cater to men is handed down from generation to generation. Some women accept the torch and others do not!

Lucy's mother became very ill and Lucy went to take care of her and spend her mother's last days with her. They talked and spent time together and Lucy's mother requested to listen to her favorite gospel hymns. They spoke about dying, that dying meant going to a better place, and how having faith confirms where you are going.

Lucy's Prince Charming Albert had heart disease and passed away. On the day that he passed, he was sitting on the carpet and Lucy was sitting with him and he was gasping for air but managed to look into Lucy's eyes. Albert told her, "It's been a wonderful journey!" Lucy looked into Albert's eyes and said, "No, it's been a great life!" Lucy then kissed the love of her life goodbye.

She still resides on her small ranch Sueno Dorado/Golden Dream with her memories and even has a life-size rag doll created by her that wears Albert's hat, clothes, and boots! She also sets a plate for Albert still, even though he is gone. She still waits on him just like her mother taught her...

Sueño
DoRAdo
RAnch

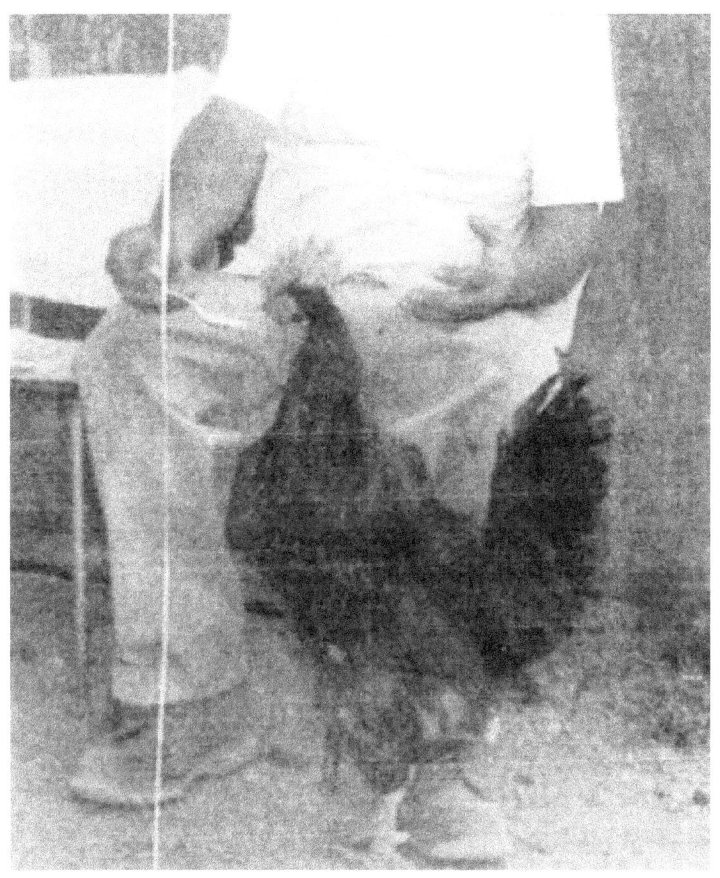

Albert feeding ice cream to his chickens.

Chickens hiccupping after eating ice cream.

Londa

"I am the fifth of nine children. Two children have passed away, one was stillborn and one died at nine months old, so there are seven of us left. There are two daughters and five brothers.

"We lived out in the country and my father worked for the railroad. I remember the wonderful memories of the freedom we had while playing, but I didn't appreciate it until we moved to town.

"We played with each other and with cousins, and it was a happy time because life was so much simpler! I truly enjoyed my childhood. We didn't have much but we were loved and happy.

"My mom was a very loving mother, hard on us when she had to be, but loving us nonetheless. She was very considerate, loyal, honest, caring, and giving. Mom was good to everybody, even the hobos that came to ask for food. One time I asked her, 'Why do you give those hobos our food?'

"She responded, 'You never say no to people that are hungry!'

"I asked, 'Why?'

"She said, 'Because it might be God wanting to see if you are a true Christian,' I will never forget that! As I got older, I under-stood what she meant. That was my mom, a heart of gold,

"I was close to my mom. I got married at sixteen years old to a military man, so I was gone most of the time. When I would come home, we talked about anything and everything! We had a beautiful mother and daughter relationship and I could feel the love and how much we had missed each other. I felt blessed that God had given me such a wonderful, loving mother!

"I can't help but be a little prejudiced about my mother. I loved everything about her! I always prayed that I would turn out like her. Her advice was always right on, even though, at the time, I didn't quite get it. Later on in life, I would remember and it would all make sense, Mom told me to never talk about anybody, and that if I could not say anything nice, do not say anything at all. She said that it would always come back to you in one way or another. Mom told me to always leave everything in God's hands.

"I remember coming home for a visit and I will never forget what she told me. She said, 'Hi Mija, when I leave this world, I can't leave you any money, jewels, or anything of value. But what I can leave you is my good name, my unconditional love, and mostly, my Catholic religion. For you see, my faith has brought me through so much!' As I write this, I can still hear her telling me this and here I sit crying.

"Little did I know that my beloved mother would pass away in a couple of months. I thank God every day for those words, as the faith she left me has helped me through so much, including the loss of my beloved mother.

"The only thing I didn't like about my mother was that she was too nice for her own good! I wish she wouldn't have let people use her. I know now that was who she was. Her life existed around my father and us children, she lived for us. I have felt many times that we didn't appreciate her as we should have, I thank my mom for giving herself to us, she gave us her all and her everything, Rest in Peace Mama.

"I learned everything from her! She was a fantastic cook and could make a delicious meal out of nothing! I truly believe it was because she cooked everything with love.

"I also remember reminding myself that I had married a military man and that even though he was my husband, he belonged to the government! Mom said, 'When they go, he has to go!!' She told me to never make him feel worse about having to leave for an assignment.

"Believe me, her advice and words of wisdom came in very handy as my husband had to leave us several times, but mom's words always came back to me and I will forever be grateful for her advice and wisdom.

"I have no daughters but I have two sons. I pray that I have taught them everything that my mom taught me. Always and fore-most, do the best you can in anything that you do. Don't ever give up on their dreams, hope and always believe in themselves.

"They can always count on me and are the most important people in my life. They are aware that they have my unconditional love. Like most mothers, I only want the best for them.

"As my mom left me these gifts, I will leave them my good name, and my faith. I lost my husband in 2014. I do have a wonderful daughter-in-law and she knows that I am here for her."

Londa hopes her three granddaughters are raised with the same wisdom passed down from her parents as hers was passed down to her mother.

"I miss everything about my mother, her advice, wisdom, smile, kindness, thought-fulness, laughter, and hugs. Most of all, I miss her waiting for me to visit her so we could enjoy each other's company and our lives! I know she will be waiting in heaven, till we meet again!

"I cook a lot of her recipes and I have taught my son some of them. My mom would do anything for anyone. I feel the same way, especially with my family. I teach my granddaughters the importance of family. I teach them that beauty doesn't last forever and they are worth more to me than all the treasures on Earth!"

Lu

"I was the youngest of three siblings. My sister is thirteen years older and my brother is eight years older.

"We lived way out in the country about twenty-five miles from town. It was a very quiet life. We went to town on Saturday for groceries and church on Sunday. I always had a dog as my best friend, and I rode the bus to school.

"My mom was a good woman. She fed us and cooked for us but was a negative person. Mom always worried about her health and going to the doctor. We fussed a lot during my teen years because I was very strong-willed. We were fairly close though. In later years, she was quite a handful! I was closer to my dad; he was easier going!

"I did love that mom could be fun when she wanted to be and would chase boys with us and let me have friends over. I just wish that she had been more positive and affectionate. Mom seldom gave praise.

"The main thing I learned from her was to pray. She taught me to pray as a little girl.

"I have two daughters, five granddaughters, two great-granddaughters, and an-other on the way! They are my life and bring so much joy! I hope I have instilled in them the importance of family and loving God. I am very close to all of them and affectionate and tell them with every communication that I love them. I have a unique relationship with each one.

Kileen

Kileen is the youngest of three siblings, and she has two older brothers. She recalls always being mad at her mother. Kileen stated that her mother's philosophy was that her husband always comes first. She also said that she and her brothers were always left out. Therefore, there was not much of a mother/daughter relationship, according to Kileen.

Kileen stated she never celebrated her birthday and "we never had a party, we just went to school and had chores."

Kileen's stepfather died and her mother moved to the state that Kileen was living in.

Kileen harbored a lot of anger and explained how short she was with her mother.

Her mother died in 2016 and to this day, Kileen misses her terribly. Kileen has a daughter and they are very dose,

"The one thing I have always taught my daughter was to take care of herself, and to never depend on anyone for anything, that way you will never owe anybody. Be strong, and never depend on a man."

Rita

Rita said that she was the eighth of nine kids. She was the middle child. Rita stated she felt left out because she felt like her mother had paid more attention to her older sister as well as her baby sister. When Rita confronted her mother about it, she was told that she didn't have any favorites. Rita said that she received all of the hand-me-downs, and her little sister got all new clothes and toys, Rita explained that she didn't appreciate the "leftovers!"

She said she truly loved her mother and describes her as being a "saint." Rita's mother was very religious and church-going. She taught Rita how to pray the Rosary, something that Rita still does to this day. Rita is also religious and is invaluable in the church. Rita had been influential in making sure her children attended church.

Rita's mom enjoyed singing "Coritos" which she described as gospel songs. Rita also sings these gospel songs that her mother had taught her to sing.

Rita recalled some unexplainable happenings in her life recently where objects moved on their own and relocated them-selves! She claims there is a ghost living in her house, and her husband does not believe her. Rita doesn't think her mother would have believed her either!

There is a story or legend about "La Llorona." This mother drowned her children and can be heard crying loudly, searching for her children along lakes or creeks.

Apparently, every town in the Hispanic culture knows about this legend and some claim that she is heard in their town also.

Her mother insisted that the family sits at the table at mealtime, all together. Rita is the same way.

Rita remembers her mother not being very affectionate, but it was understood that she and her siblings were loved. Her mother was a great cook, while Rita states that she herself is a horrible cook!

Rita's mother worked hard and some-times worked two jobs. She vowed, "She would work in nothing but her underwear to provide for her children." Rita is a social worker and she loves her job.

Her mother was not educated but she was still very smart and encouraged Rita and her siblings to obtain an education. She wanted to make sure that Rita's sisters would be able to take care of themselves and not be dependent upon any man.

Apparently, there were girls who were mistreated by their husbands and Rita's mother wanted to make sure her daughters would be able to independently take care of themselves.

Rita is close to her siblings and enjoys getting together with one of her sisters. The youngest sister even went to a San Antonio Spurs basketball game with them on one occasion.

Rita described her younger sister as envious, and doesn't understand why. "I like to live in my tiny home in the area I live in. My younger sister had no children and has no idea what it is like to have memories of my children growing up here!"

In case you're wondering if Rita's father was in her life, he was. He spoiled Rita's mother and catered to her every whim! Rita said her father definitely knew her mother was the boss! Rita recalls how her parents were non-affectionate with one another, except for when her father died. Rita described her mother as being in denial and picking up her husband's hand, placing it on her cheek and saying, "He's not dead, his hand is still warm!" "Mother gave up when dad died, and started going down and later died."

Rita continues to be supportive of her children, and affectionate, and they know they can talk to her about anything. Rita is close to her daughter and sons. She has taught her daughter to be strong, kind, and independent.

Mary Alice

Mary Alice was the only child. "My mother hated me! She had me when she was four-teen years old. My parents fought back and forth and I finally went to live with my mom's mother (my grandmother). Later though, my parents picked me back up and took me home.

Mary Alice said that her parents continued to fight off and on. According to Mary Alice, her parents separated and her father moved out of the house. She stated her mother began living with a man who abused Mary Alice emotionally, verbally, as well as physically with his fists and his belts.

When Mary Alice was twelve, she recalls how she was forced to stay in the closet for days. Her mother allowed the abuse, and would also abuse Mary Alice if she attempted to stop the boyfriend from beating her mother! When this occurred, they would both take turns beating her.

Mary Alice's parents reunited and her mother never apologized. Her father was aware of the abuse and turmoil that Mary Alice had endured, and he apologized to her then and continues to verbalize how sorry he is for not intervening when he should have.

Mary Alice gave birth to her first son at just fifteen years old. Her mother immediately took over and raised her grandson as if he was her own. Mary Alice had no say so, and she knew better than to argue about it. She was still so young.

Mary Alice said that her mother spoiled her son and as he was growing up and getting into trouble, her mother enabled him. Although her son was aware that Mary Alice was his biological mother, he still called his grandmother "Mom." This occurred until Mary Alice herself did some growing up and began to stand up to both her son and her mother. Mary Alice reminded both of them that she was his mother and that her mother was actually his grandmother!

Things were not perfect after that, but Mary Alice was finally able to voice her opinions and frustrations. Mary Alice ended up having three more children, and bad relationships. Her mother also continued to enable her grandson despite Mary Alice having verbal altercations with her. A year ago, Mary Alice's son died. Both Mary Alice and her mother were distraught, and the relationship began to deteriorate before it had a chance to heal.

Mary Alice said that her mother began to bribe her other son into seeing life her way by showering him with gifts and enabling him just like she had with Mary Alice's first son. When Mary Alice became aware of what was transpiring, she put her foot down and confronted her mother and reminded her that Mary Alice was the mother and she was the grandmother.

Mary Alice stated that her mother went through a lot, becoming a mother so young, having abusive relationships and so much anger. Mary Alice tells her mother she for-gives her often. Her mother, unfortunately, does not respond.

Mary Alice is proud of her children and admits that although she is not a perfect mother, her children, now adults, know that they are loved. She has been in therapy for years and still struggles with depression and PTSD. Mary Alice explained forgiveness is food for her soul.

Mary Alice has one daughter and they are very close, and she has taught her to be independent and true to herself.

Annie

"I'm the oldest of four siblings. Growing up wasn't easy in my home, as I came from an abusive environment. People often ask me how my relationship with my mom is. I can honestly say, 'I don't know, as we don't speak to one another.'

"My parents got divorced when I was young. My mother told the court she did not want us, so I feel that my dad had no choice but to take us!

"Even then, we ended up moving in with my grandparents, my dad's parents. Every time it was my mother's turn for visitation, my brothers and I would cry hysterically asking, 'Do we have to go?'

"The reason we didn't like to go with my mom was that she was abusive. She moved around a lot, gambled, and used our names for obtaining credit. My siblings and I had bad credit before we were even teenagers! Mom was always in and out of prison, and I was so unhappy as a child.

"I met the man I would later marry when I was only eleven years old. I noticed what a real family looked like, His parents were still together and they were good to me at the beginning. His siblings were close and they all ate at the table like a family and had conversations about everyday things or issues. It was then that I realized how dysfunctional my family life was, and that being beaten and molested were not normal things.

"I became a mom at fifteen. I have learned a lot from my mom. I learned how not to be a parent.

"My mom blames everyone else for her bad times and wrongdoings. She lives in the past and not in the present. My siblings and I don't have any kind of relationship with my mom, except for my younger brother and my little sister who came way after the divorce of my parents. My dad didn't know about her until I had to contact CPS on my mom when I found my sister with no electricity or food in the fridge, and all alone for three days!

"It was then that I completely shut my mom out of my life. My dad ended up get-ting custody of my sister, but my mom and she didn't get along so my parents signed her over to me when she was sixteen.

"I lived with my ex-husband's family from the age of fourteen and married him when I was twenty. After we married, the marriage only lasted a couple of months, and I already had two children. My youngest is from another relationship.

My ex was in boot camp and didn't want me to have the baby. He offered me money to abort her and since I was going through an ugly custody battle with my ex, I saw this time in my life where no one wanted me to have her, no one would want her and I could finally have something that was mine, and mine alone! I could love her and she would love me in return. Having my daughter literally saved my life.

"I was very suicidal after the separation from my ex and being raped and molested. I began mutilating myself. I overdosed and when I woke up in the hospital, I found out I was pregnant with my youngest, and that's when I knew I needed to fight for my daughter and not put my children through this. 1 almost died and that is why I say she saved my life!

"The moment I found out I was going to be a mom again, I changed overnight.

"She and I are very close and she lives with me. My other daughter and I began to mend our relationship when she became a mom. She and I talk now, and I'm grateful to be a grandma, thanks to her!

"I love my kids very much. I didn't know how to express affection because my mom never showed us any. So, when people say it comes naturally when you become a mom, that's not entirely true. It didn't come naturally to me, so my therapist helps us with our bonding. My daughter's dad rejecting her has really hurt her, but she has me, and we have each other.

"I have very few people that care about me, so I don't take anything for granted. The one true person that has been with me through it all has been the Lord above!

"I almost lost my faith after the horrible accident of my fiancé. He was the humblest man I ever met, and helped me raise my daughter from the time she was two months old. We were together for thirteen years until the horrible burn accident, I began to lose faith completely and resorted to bad things and bad people. I couldn't believe something so terrible could happen to good people.

"I eventually restored my faith though, thanks to my dad, coworkers, and the Bible.

"My sister that I raised is studying law and makes me proud!
It changed our relationship from sisters to mother/daughter!
My siblings and I are making our own traditions and living
life as best we can."

Ester

Ester was the second of two siblings, and she is two years younger than her brother.

Ester recalls her childhood as being centered around her parents' business. Owning their own business was very time-consuming and stressful.

As a small child Ester remembers being at the office daily before she became of school age. According to Ester, she and her brother were their parents' "marketing team." She described how her brother and she created an assembly line where they would fold, address, and direct the mail pieces to help build the parents' business.

Ester stated, "As I grew up and started going to school, I began to understand how busy my parents would get. We would get left at school, sometimes for over an hour after release time to be picked up."

Ester recalled how it was usually the dad that would pick her up. He would take them back to the office after they would "grab a bite to eat." She and her brother would work on their homework and play with the office/neighborhood kids. Sometimes though, they would cross the street to the convenience store to play video games or just hang out in the back office,

Ester remembers that when she was between the ages of ten and eleven, her brother was between the ages of twelve and fourteen, and their parents finally decided that they were old enough to be home by themselves. That is where they wanted to be anyway!

Ester said it was difficult for her to understand why her mother was not around much and would arrive home late when Ester was already asleep. She also recalls how her parents were late to school functions or did not show up at all, and how disappointing it was.

Ester said she got along with her mother because if she disobeyed, she would get in trouble. Ester recalls holidays being stressful. She said Thanksgiving was celebrated with friends mostly out of town. Ester re-members rarely gathering with extended family,

Christmas was the most stressful because it was work for her mother to cook and prepare for the company arriving for the annual Christmas Eve gathering, she said.

Ester stated that as she grew older, she understood a little more about her parents' schedule. She is now a mother herself and in the same line of work as her mom and realizes how challenging it can be to balance life! Ester said she is a little more under-standing and forgiving to her mother. She said she doesn't know how her mom did it all!

Ester stated she is grateful to her mom and that she was close by to help her with her kids when they were younger. They continue to have a good mother/daughter relationship.

Evelyn

"I believe a mother-daughter relationship is very crucial in a girl's life. When I was younger, I didn't appreciate my mom the way I should have. I know now that if I would have shown her the appreciation she deserves, our relationship would have been a lot less rocky. A bond with your mother should be the closest bond you have!

"Despite our disagreements, my mom had always been my best friend. Growing up, my mom and I bumped heads, but it was mainly because of her relationships, I always felt that she deserved more, and it always angered me to watch her settle.

"I hate to see my momma hurt, so eventually, I just didn't want to see her with anyone. I started to feel as though no man was deserving of her. I have a lot of mother's traits, which is why I feel we bumped heads as much as we did! We are alike in so many ways, and the main trait we have in common is stubbornness. We are both so stubborn that it's crazy!

"Not too long ago, we got into one of the biggest altercations of our relationship. We were both going through so much at the time, and instead of communicating, we just blew up on one another. Momma had just lost her job, her car started messing up, she has four kids to take care of on her own, plus my brother is in prison,

"We went days without communicating and those days turned into months. It felt like a lifetime. We were both talking to people we shouldn't have been talking to.

"Everyone was twisting up our words, and it was making the situation worse!

"After that, everything went downhill. I cried every day for a while. I felt like I had no one, and I thought the world had turned against me. It was the lowest point in my life at the time.

"My mom was my best friend and I just could not believe what people were saying that she was saying about me! Eventually, I just made up my mind to not have anything more to do with her. I was hurt. I was experiencing stuff that I never thought I would go through without my mom! I truly didn't know how hard life would be without her.

"To top it off, everybody made it sound like she was doing perfectly fine with-out me. This made me furious because I couldn't understand how she was living life while I felt like I was drowning. The reality is that if I had spoken to my mom, I would have known that she was having trouble with the situation as well. I eventually found out that she had attempted suicide. I didn't know until months later when my sister informed me.

"When I saw her at my high school graduation, she looked like she wasn't get-ting any rest, and had lost so much weight. It broke my heart all over again! To know that I made my mom feel like her life wasn't worth living, it broke me. It still breaks my heart to this day to know that I hurt the woman who always made sure my siblings and I had clothes on our backs, shoes on our feet, and food on the table.

"It never mattered how hard life got, she always made a way for us! It shattered me because I just should have talked to her instead of being selfish. It could have pre-vented a lot of strife between her and I.

"When we finally did sit down and talk about the whole situation, there were a lot of tears, and we discovered that everything had been blown out of proportion, and if we had just gone to each other and talked instead of talking to everyone else, things wouldn't have escalated to that point. We could've prevented so much hurt!

"I love my mom more than anybody in this world. We may bump heads or have disagreements, but at the end of the day, I know no one will have my back like my mom. I have learned so much from her. She taught me to be understanding towards others in any situation because you never know what other people are battling. I continuously pray to be the type of woman/mother that my mom is. I know now that it's a blessing to have such a wonderful mother to guide and protect you in this crazy world! My mom may not always agree with my decisions and I may not always agree with hers, but we have learned to be understanding towards one another. We will always try to be honest with each other, no matter whose feelings get hurt because, in the end, we are daughter and mother."

Laura

Laura is the middle child of three siblings, all girls. Her mother was a stay-at-home mom and her father worked. He was away from home most of the time. Laura was close to her mother but did not have a father/daughter bond or relationship since her dad was always gone. Her mother cooked, cleaned, and was submissive to her husband.

Laura informed me how much she regrets not having paid attention when her mother was preparing delicious meals, especially during the holidays! Laura said during the holidays her mother cooked American and Filipino food and invited family and friends, and had a wonderful time! Laura was taught to respect her elders and family. Laura was grateful for her mother being supportive and wanting her and her sisters to become educated.

However, Laura expressed that her mother did not give them good advice when it came to relationships and marriage. According to Laura, they were advised to go along with men's wishes and to "stroke their egos." This advice had worked for her mother and told her that as long as they had a man who had lucrative employment and a good education, "Go along with him." Laura admitted she had made a few poor choices and learned from them. She later realized that her mother had given her poor advice.

Laura remained close to her mother; and eventually, her parent returned to the Philippines, and they both passed away there. Laura is happy and fondly remembers the good times. She is independent and believes that a relationship/marriage should be as close to 50/50 as possible. She knows it doesn't always work out this way, but she remains her own person.

Laurie

Laurie was the oldest of two children. Her parents divorced when she was five, and she lived with her mom, who was attending college, Laurie remembers having to move three times until her mother remarried. Laurie said they lived on a ranch while growing up and she graduated high school in the small town where they lived.

Laurie said her mother was married three times to men who were different from her mom. She said her mother supported her all through her childhood, sports, and Laurie's love for horses.

Holidays were split between her mother and grandparents, her dad and his parents and therefore, there were lots of presents! Laurie remembered how much fun Christ-mas was and playing with her cousins. She described her relationship with her mother as close, and as being "best friends." Laurie said her mother has accompanied her on trips to Ireland, England, and Mexico, on cruises, and functions with horse trips.

Her mother supported Laurie through obtaining two degrees and has taught her to be independent and to never settle for second best. They haven't always agreed on everything, but got the issue resolved and moved on! They remain close even though they don't see each other often. When they do get together, they enjoy going shopping and spending time together.

Dee

Dee was the fifth child born of six children in total. "I was the first girl and my sibling that followed was also a girl.

"I don't have many memories of how I grew up! I can only refer to pictures for a memory boost.

"We lived on farmlands because my father worked the land for the owners."

Dee described how as children; they were expected to work the fields. They were expected to do chores such as picking cot-ton and hoeing weeds.

The mother had a second-grade education, and she was very good at math. Since she was also able to read and write, she was in charge of the "Braceros" that were hired to come and pick the cotton. Her oldest brother taught Dee and her siblings how to speak English. She said they all forgot how to speak Spanish but understood it.

Dee and her siblings rode the bus to school and the neighbors would scream slurs at them because they were Mexicans! They later all became friends and would go to Dee's house to eat fresh, hot tortillas! Dee describes herself as an introvert up until high school.

She stated her mother was a brave but submissive woman, but she was also dominated by her husband (Dee's dad).

Dee's parents would sing in the church and her mother would compose songs for special church functions and Sunday mass.

Dee stated her mother paid the bills and did the banking. Her mother later worked at the military base cleaning homes and preparing them for military families. "My mother worked and was exposed to so many harsh chemicals and developed a dis-ease called systemic sclerosis."

"My mother balanced work and family well." Dee described the mother as having a good work ethic and being dependable. Dee described how her father would not take them to the doctor or a dentist and how she almost died from her appendix bursting. It was then that her father allowed her to go see the doctor!

Dee's siblings began leaving home and living out on their own. For several years Dee believed her mother was okay even though her father was domineering. The mother never complained and pretended everything was fine. Dee described having a hard life growing up with a domineering father and a submissive mother.

Her father was against Dee going off to college, but agreed to let her go, and informed her he would not assist her financially. But Dee had her mother's blessings and said her mother would send her $5.00 whenever she could. This meant so much to Dee. When Dee would come home to visit, her mother would prepare her favorite fideos (Mexican pasta). Dee was thankful for her mother's support.

Dee's father passed away and her mother wanted her children to see their father in a good way. Dee and her mother became closer and would do things together, going out to eat, shopping, and Dee found out just how unhappy and mistreated her mom had been throughout her married life.

Dee admired her mother but vowed she would never allow a man to control or dominate her.

Her mother became gravely ill and Dee spent quality time with her mother. Dee described her mother as a strong woman and said she learned how to be loving and forgiving and has taught her two daughters how to be independent and stand their ground. She is also supportive and approving of their dreams and goals. Dee is an educator, teacher, retired, and continues to enjoy teaching pre-K children.

Bree

Bree was the firstborn. "Life and growing up was fun, active, and there was never a dull moment! We had plenty of extracurricular activities. My mom was strict and made sure we knew right from wrong. We were disciplined when it was needed.

"Holidays were always about family and were spent with family. My mom taught me how to sew, crochet, hand stitch, cook, and most of all, how to survive with very little.

"My mom and I got along very well, and still do. We are very close, I loved the way I could be open with my mom, how close we were, and how thankful I was to her for teaching me so many useful things! The only thing that I didn't like, though, was when she was disappointed or angry with me, "I have four daughters, and I am teaching them responsibility, hygiene, how to cook, clean, and how to be respectful to elders and to everyone."

Diane

Diane is the middle child of six siblings. She described her family as "the Waltons"!

Diane said that she had a great child-hood and a praying mother that was filled with faith no matter what was going on. Diane stated that she and her mother have always been close.

"Holidays were awesome because we would go to church at midnight on Christ-mas Eve (Misa de Gallo)." She recalled how special that was and that her mother would prepare hot chocolate, capirotada (Mexican pudding), and the traditional bunuelos (bread). After the meal, the family would open Christmas gifts.

Diane's mother taught her to pray, cook, clean and have faith. Her mother has dementia now, but she still remembers to pray and prays for others as well. "My mom is an angel, and loves everybody!" Diane admires her mother for her strength, faith, and love.

Diane has one daughter who currently resides with her and her mother. Diane said that she loves the closeness they all share.

She has taught her daughter to keep the faith, even though the storms in life. Diane continues her faith and shares it through social media and sometimes her mother prays for others to have special blessings on Facebook!

Tina

Tina is the baby of two siblings. She explained that she was an "accident" and she has a brother that is sixteen years older than her.

Tina said she grew up on a street filled with kids her age and her parents socialized with them.

Being so much younger than her brother and cousins, though, Tina said she was alone at family events. "I enjoyed being with my friends more, but I think that's normal!"

Tina describes her mom as being a strong woman and a strong disciplinarian. "She was a teacher and sadly had a kid when she almost had her life back! She looked like Dorothy from The Golden Girls!! We got along, but because her hormones were going out, and mine were coming in, it sometimes made for a lot of discord during the teenage years. We got closer when the grandkids arrived.

"Holidays were the best time! It was one of the few times treats were allowed in the house! I got to experience holidays with the 50s and 60s decorations and some that were handmade. I like the nostalgic look be-cause of those days!

"My mom hummed and whistled when she was in a good mood. I loved those days! They were rare, but that's one of my favorite memories, hearing that tune"

Tina expressed that her mother always favored her brother, so she also favored Tina's son quite a bit. Tina said she also regrets that her mother did not give her brother "tougher love."

"I just wanted her to be happier. I figured if she found happiness, she would enjoy more time with me." Tina said she learned to cook from her mom and how to keep and make her home look nice.

"I have one daughter who is my exact opposite! She taught her some cooking.

"She's better than me so she learns a lot on her own. I taught her some driving.

We're still working on that!"

Licha

Licha is second to the oldest of two brothers and two sisters. She remembers having a beautiful time with her siblings and said they had a lot of fun times,

Holidays were special for Licha and her siblings. They got together with all of their family and celebrated traditional customs of Mexican food and festivities. Interacting with her many "Primos," or cousins, was simply the best!

"I got along well with my mother when I was little, but things became harder for me as a teenager. My mother was very strict, but I still behaved and respected her because she was my mom! My mom was a very serious person, but could be reasonable and nice when she wanted to! We loved her the way she was. Mom was very strong and did not show affection. It was understood that we were loved and had the essentials that we needed. My mom was the boss of the house and even my dad knew it. He was very loving and affectionate.

"Mom taught me how to cook, make tortillas, and how to take care of myself.

Mom taught me to be respectful to elders and others. I am affectionate to my two daughters and have passed on my Hispanic traditions, culture, and holidays. It is up to them to continue the traditions handed down from my mother to me and from me to them. They can also create their own traditions! I have taught my daughters to be respectful and independent, and to not rely on anybody."

Cristina

Cristina is the oldest of two siblings. She said her mother is pretty easy to get along with, even though she was very strict and expected respect. "My mother just wanted the best for us!" Cristina said growing up was normal and smooth. She described how her parents were partners even in parenting. "I loved everything about my mother!"

Cristina expressed how her mother worked outside the home and managed to take care of the house and them. "I loved that she was able to balance work and us!"

Cristina learned how to cook Menudo and pozole and keep a clean house from her mother and also how to take care of herself.

Cristina remembers spending holidays at home and her mother preparing the traditional Mexican favorite dishes of tamales, Menudo, pozole, and pastries. Friends and family gathered at the home and enjoyed eating and socializing.

In the Hispanic culture, there is a coming-of-age birthday celebration that occurs when a young girl turns fifteen years of age. It is like a Sweet Sixteen party or debutante party, but it is called a quinceanera in the Hispanic culture, Cristina happily described her quinceanera 15th birthday celebration as a beautiful occasion and felt honored for her parents to present her with a beautiful memory.

Cristina remembers celebrating with a mass, reception, dance, and a beautiful cake.

It is tradition to have fifteen attendants, male and female, to represent your fifteen years. These attendants are called the quinceanera's court, La Marcha is a celebration march that is also traditional for quinceanera, weddings, and anniversaries, and the court creates different designs while they are marching. The quinceanera and her escort are in front and follow the guide of the Marcha coordinators, a male, and a female.

Another traditional quinceanera dance is The Mariposa or The Butterfly. The quinceanera stands in the middle and the court creates a circle around her. A beautiful song, "La Mariposa," is played and the quinceanera sways softly back and forth, and the court attendants also move to the music. Each male attendant then dances with the quinceanera and returns to his place in the circle to dance with his escort.

The dance becomes a beautiful soft waltz!

Cristina praised her mother for the planning and coordination of her quinceanera and unforgettable celebration. Cristina also said that her mother continues to be active, and still manages to balance home and work. Cristina has two sons and she is teaching them how to be respectable and kind just as her mother taught her.

W.M. Parris

W.M. is the first of four children. She describes her relationship with her mom as "complex." There were times when she got along with her mom and many times when she did not. W.M. described being raised in a culture where you did not verbally disagree with your elders. "The outside appearance of getting along with my mom is probably what most people saw, but internally, there were so many times that I disagreed with her and it was just safer for me to stay quiet and pretend that everything was good.

"Growing up, life was somewhat chaotic. I lived close to my aunts and other Native American families. The land that we lived on was small but was thought of as a small reservation, To this day, I miss it so much! I never really knew what I would encounter from one day to the next.

"We lived in extreme poverty and had to deal with everything that came with it. Needless to say, I knew at a very early age that I was not going to live that way forever.

"The holidays were pretty low-key. On Thanksgiving, we ate turkey and a few side items but it was not anything like I had seen on TV, or like the "more privileged" kids at school spoke about. We didn't decorate for holidays except during Christmas when we did chop down our own Christmas tree and maybe had one gift under the tree.

"There were many years when I remember that one gift was from my aunt who would crochet for all the kids, a pair of socks or a hat. It may not have been what our hearts desired, but it was still better than nothing!

"I liked when my mom was sober because she made me feel like she somewhat cared for me! I disliked my mom's erratic, violent, hurtful, disgusting behavior when she was drunk, and that was eighty percent of the time. I would have liked my mom to be more caring like other parents, to have interacted with me, take me to the library, to be more interested in my schoolwork and in the athletic programs that I participated in."

W.M. said that she longed for a well-balanced meal and that in school, she ate the free meal. She said the plain cheese sandwich she would take to school tasted much better!

W.M. stated that she learned more of how not to be, than how to be, from her mom. She also said that she did learn not to allow herself to be abused physically by any man, or not to smoke because it damages the lungs. She learned not to drink alcohol to the point of becoming addicted. She also described how she would not ever depend on others to completely provide for her be-cause then they would hold all of the power!

W.M. said she definitely learned from her mom to watch her tongue because "Words cut deeper than any physical pain and last longer," and remembers her mother's alcoholic rages towards her. Ac-cording to W.M., she knew the parameters that she needed to work within and she realized her mother was sick and needed her help, not her judgment.

Mia

Mia was the oldest of three children. She had both a sister and a brother. She was close to her siblings and father, but not so much to her mother. It was painful for Mia to recount her experience, but she wanted to share it with others.

Mia recalls having a hard time growing up, and at the age of ten years old, she be-came the second mother to her siblings. Mia states that this was because her mother had a psychotic breakdown. Her mother had been hiding her mental illness so well. Mia bathed, fed, and tucked her siblings in at bedtime. She was not sure what her mother was doing; all she remembers is that it was expected and very much needed.

Mia's father traveled with his employment and had been in the service, and he wasn't around as Mia and her siblings longed for him. Mia did not want her father to know how mistreated they were, and she had been warned not to, and her mother forbade any discussion about what was going on. Mia's father had no idea of how she and her siblings were living and were being treated by their mother. Mia continued to take care of her siblings and did not want her father to know as he was a loving and hard-working man.

Mia, at twelve years old, and her sister, who was six at the time, cleaned the whole house and did all of the laundry. Being home-schooled, Mia did not have a social life.

Mia's mother expected them to complete a certain number of pages daily. They didn't see their mother much while they were working on their schoolwork.

My mom was the authority in the house. I was more worried about upsetting her than anything else. She did always seem very worried about letting us out of her sight."

Mia said her sister and she were six years apart and they joked about being twins since they were inseparable.

"I loved being a second mom to my siblings. When I was ten, I was the one who took care of them. I rocked my brother to sleep and put him down for naps and bedtime. I read him stories, changed his di-apers, fed them both, and took care of them while they were sick. My childhood until I was thirteen was idyllic. When I was a teenager, it was tough, because my mother became extremely controlling. We did not realize it at the time, but I think her mental illness was beginning to manifest.

"Since we were homeschooled, we were very isolated. My mother would sometimes allow us the rare friendship here and there but then she would sabotage and end them." Mia explained that her mother was resistant to any talk of growing up. "I do believe that she wanted to keep us at home indefinitely."

"I begged for a bra when it started be-coming embarrassing. She bought me one that was too small for me.

"When I was 21 and still living at home, she told me not to talk to boys/men at my job. My mom did not want to allow any relationships, male or female. She felt that I learned bad habits while becoming a teenager, like smiling too big."

Mia said that her mother didn't talk to her about puberty, however, she did tell Mia about all the gruesome details of her own ectopic pregnancy and surgery when Mia was thirteen.

"I didn't leave home at a young age for several reasons. My mother was incredibly verbally and emotionally abusive. She lectured me anywhere from 1 to 3 hours a day about how bad a person I was and how I was not a true Christian. I honestly didn't know that I could leave. I also stayed because I could not leave my sister exposed to the same devastating, abusive behavior that I had to endure! As long as I was there, she was safe. I did finally leave for college, but only because it was a life-or-death situation for me. I made sure that my sister went to college at 17, and I was only able to convince my mom when I told her that I had made arrangements for my sister to be my roommate.

"I've always been so close to my dad. He was the one who would gently detangle my hair when I was a child. I could tell him anything except what my mom was doing to me because she forbade it and she had control of us all day. He was always so loving then and still is today. I learned more from him about life than I ever did from my mom.

"I do tend to ramble and talk a lot like my mom. My mom and I don't have a relationship, because her mental illness ended that. She feels that I am responsible for her misfortune. She says I am trying to annihilate the family. There is no reasoning behind that. When we do talk, she invariably starts yelling at me like she used to and I fall into the same sense of being powerless all over again. My husband actually has to remind me that I don't have to tolerate that anymore!"

Iris Ann

The baby of three children, Iris Ann was the only girl with two older brothers. She had a good lifestyle since Dad was a CEO of a re-finery, and Mom was a stay-at-home mom, although she had been a registered nurse before becoming an airline stewardess.

They were even members of the country club. Her mother also taught Ann how to cook, bake bread, and clean the house from the time she was little, even though they also had a cook, a maid, and a housekeeper.

When Ann was 22 years old, her mother began to talk to her about her wanting Ann to be taken care of. The parents had resources, money, and prestige, but both became alcoholics and had health problems. Ann's father died, and then her mother passed away soon after Ann had gotten married. Her parents had also made sure that Ann and her brothers had trust funds, etc.

Ann loved her mother. They could talk about anything and her mother was a lot of fun. Once, her mother bought silk sheets for Ann and Ann slid off the bed and hit her head! They both found it very hilarious.

No one could babysit the children but her mom's sister. "Other people thought we were spoiled but we had only one TV and we had no phones in our room.

"Mom cooked and prepared food for the holidays. Christmas Eve was for the parents, and Christmas Day was for the kids."

Iris and her mother had a great relationship when she returned from boarding school. Iris was gone from home from the 8th grade till she finished high school. Iris did come home for the holidays and summer vacation,

Iris's mom loved to dress up, and loved jewelry and shoes. Iris Ann, on the other hand, liked to wear casual clothes and preferred comfortable shoes and selective jewelry.

Iris's mom loved to cook and even though she had a cook, she also shared the kitchen and enjoyed preparing meals and pastries with the cook. Iris also loves being in the kitchen and preparing delicious meals, especially during the holidays, Al-though, Iris does not like for anyone to be in her kitchen, or to help her cook! She said she has OCD (obsessive-compulsive disorder) and prefers to do things herself.

Iris's mom loved to socialize and entertain friends and family members that she was close to. She said she is a little like her mom, but mostly she is her own person. Iris is thankful that her mom taught her to be self-sufficient and strong. She has no children.

Louise

Louise was the third of seven siblings. She also recalls how she and her sisters had breast cancer at the same time! Louise was the first, followed by the middle sister six months later, and six months after that, her youngest sister found out that she had breast cancer! Louise remembered how her mother cried every time she saw them, which was quite often, as she accompanied them to chemotherapy.

Louise was in a cancer study group and did not take the chemical chemotherapy.

She took pills and if they caused side effects, they would get changed. To this day, she has an irregular heartbeat and had suffered a light stroke while on the pill therapy, and has very thin hair. Louise's other two sisters were on chemotherapy. Louise and her mother picked them up and took them to chemotherapy. They went on different days of the week.

"My mother was very supportive and strong for us," recalls Louise, "and we stayed strong for her."

Louise's mother was supportive of Louise's choice of husband. Her own marriage had not been very fruitful, as Louise's daddy was an alcoholic. Her father didn't work, and Louise's mother often worked two jobs to support her seven children.

Louise's mother was a kind and hard-working woman. She made sure that the children were clean, fed, and respectful. All four of her female siblings and her two male siblings were close to their mother and she had a special relationship with each one of her children.

Despite her father not working, and drinking daily, though, he was still considered the head of the household.

Louise recalls the day her boyfriend asked her to go to a dance out of town.

Louise sadly explained to the boyfriend that she was not allowed to date, much less go to a dance, and certainly not out of town! But the boyfriend was very insistent and brave! He told Louise "I'll take care of it." That evening, the boyfriend knocks on the door, her father answers, and there is her boyfriend, standing there," all cool and collected." Louise's daddy asks, "Who are you and what do you want?" Her boyfriend introduces himself and extends his hand, but that was not reciprocated!

As her boyfriend is explaining why he is there, Louise's father tells him that, number one, Louise is not allowed to date. Number two, she is not allowed to go to dances, and number three, especially not out of town! Her boyfriend right away explained his "honorable" intentions. Louise in the mean-time, is hiding behind the bedroom door and shaking from fright!

All of a sudden, her dad says, "Ok, tell you what. Why don't you get back in your car and go around the block slowly and I'll have my answer." The boyfriend gets back in his car, drives slowly around the block, gets out of the car, and knocks on the door: Her dad asks him to come in, this time asking him to sit. He calls Louise out and tells her that she can go but has to be home by midnight.

Louise added, "Just like Cinderella!"

Louise's mother was working and just shook her head when she found out that Louise was going to a dance out of town with a guy and laughed at what had transpired.

Louise has a loving relationship with her mother and siblings. She was proud of her mother and respected her for being so hard working and had graduated from high school and been on the volleyball team! She also had some college and was very intelligent.

Louise married a handsome and well-educated man, and since she is also educated, her mother definitely approved of him. Louise reminded him right before the wedding that she would put up with being poor, but that she would most definitely not tolerate cheating, womanizing, alcoholism, or being physically, emotionally, verbally or sexually abused.

Louise has raised a son and a daughter and has taught them to be strong and independent. Her daughter is smart, educated and a little like her grandmother, a lot like Louise, and totally herself!

Tillie

Tillie was the baby of four girls. She had never really bonded with her mother and didn't get along with her sisters, Tillie was starved for her mother's love, but her daddy gave her love and attention and spoiled all three of the older girls as well. Tillie's father also spoiled her mother and it became a competition!

Her mother was born and raised in Mexico, and was "privileged," according to Tillie. While growing up, her mother would play her and her sisters against one another and also against their father. Tillie stated, "My mother didn't want to share attention." Tillie's mother wanted all of the attention for herself.

Growing up, Tillie said that her mom was very stern, not to mention physically and verbally abusive to the girls while growing up. Thankfully, her dad was quite the opposite! He had patience and approved of Tillie and her sisters' typical teenage lifestyles.

As Tillie grew up, married, and had her own children, she continued to want to develop some kind of mother/daughter relationship. Tillie's sisters were also married and had families of their own, Tillie and her sisters had not grown close or had formed any kind of relationship.

On the contrary, though, there was a lot of sibling rivalry, all instigated by her very own mother! Her mother would call each of her daughters and tell them that the other sister was a "rich bitch," and how much they hated that one particular sister that she was talking about at the time. The sisters would then stay mad at each other.

Therefore, there was not much family- together time or celebrating during the holidays. Tillie's mother would taunt her daughters and say that she had four "locas" and that one was worse than the others! Her mother seemed to know everybody's business and the neighbor's "hanky panky!"

Her mother got breast cancer and Tillie recalls how she wanted pity after Tillie's daddy died. She called Tillie to come and see her. So, Tillie droves for hours and when she arrived, her mother berated her, so she drove home. On another occasion, Tillie drove out of town to see her and she refused to even open the door! So, Tillie droves back home once again.

She said that communication with her family became almost non-existent. Tillie explained that she speaks to one sister only. She also came to the realization that although her mother was never properly. Tillie believes that she was depressed, suffered from OCD, and harbored a lot of anger that was unfortunately directed at her daughters.

Tillie was there for her mother when she became very ill. Since then, Tillie and her sisters have become closer and are finally forming a sisterly bond with each other. Tillie has no daughters but is a friend, a good listener, and a great advisor to her friends.

Nancy

Nancy was the fifth of twelve siblings. Her father lived a polygamous lifestyle. Nancy had a stepmom. She considers the children that her stepmom brought into the home as her siblings as well.

Later on, though, more children were discovered since her father committed in-fidelity to both her mom and her stepmom. Actually, Nancy's stepmom was brought into the home when Nancy's mom was still pregnant with her, and before her father and stepmother were married. Nancy stated that she was close to her mother, stepmom, and her siblings.

"My mom was my world," Nancy said.

"She was my mom. She would be firm when it was needed, but she was my best friend as well. She was a very funny lady, so her humor was my favorite part of her. She had no enemies at all. She really was perfect in almost every way. I wish she would have been healthier and more led all of us in a healthier way."

Her mother became a diabetic and later on, Nancy also became a diabetic as well,

It was hard for Nancy to be living in the lifestyle of her father and the polygamous environment and infidelity.

"My mom made holidays as much fun as she could with as little as she had. But we didn't remember the presents, only the family time. The family time, the love and hope that surrounded us in that moment in time!

"There are so many things that my mom taught me. But the best advice that she gave me was how to be the mom that she taught me to become. She taught me to love my babies no matter what happens, good, bad, or ugly. They're part of you, and you will have in return what you put in. The same advice Nancy says she will share with her three daughters as well.

Otila

Otila stated she was the second to the oldest of four siblings. Otila was close to her mother. She said her mother loved being a stay-at-home mom and loved giving orders.

Otila described how her mother had a list of what each one's chore was each day. Otila said that her mother loved to cook. She ex-pressed how her mother loved to dress up and how her father liked it also! Otila did mention how she was a daddy's girl also.

And that her mother paid all the bills and did the bank dealings as well. Otila said that she had a beautiful upbringing and that she and her siblings couldn't have asked for a better mother.

Holidays were awesome according to Otila. Otila said that Christmas and birthdays were especially awesome. She described her birthday as a fun time, and how she would get everything that she had asked for, plus more.

In November, Otila's mother would make a fruit cake that she would add some rum to and they would have it for the holidays. Otila said that they celebrated Christmas on the 24th of December. Her mother, being very sociable, Otila stated, would invite family and friends over for a special soup. She jokingly called it "Turtle Soup." Her mother also had turkey with all of the trimmings. Christmas gifts were everything that they had asked for. Otila also received double gifts because Christmas is also her birthday.

After the 29th of December, there would be another big fiesta because it was her parents' anniversary. Otila said her mother, of course, invited everybody. Otila said her mother taught her to be responsible, respectful to her elders, be friendly, and to cherish friendships, and to lastly remain close to family.

Her mother had one request for Otila be-fore she got married. Her mother told her to never let her know if she and her husband were having marital problems because she was her mother, and it would make her dis-respect her husband, and the chances were that Otila and her husband would probably make up, but as her mother, she would harbor ill feelings still. Otila said that she is grateful for her happy life and upbringing, and especially for her upbringing.

Jana

Jana said she was the third of four siblings, One male, and three females. Her mom was always working, but Jana stated that they understood that there was little to no help from their father. As she became older, she understood he did step up some.

Jana stated her mother has always provided for them as best as she can. She expressed how awesome and amazing her mother is. Jana admits that she and her mother have ups and downs, but for the most part, they have a good understanding of one another. Jana stated that her mother has always given her good advice and also for her siblings. She recalls having the best holidays filled with much laughter, love, and joy. Jana says that she would not change anything. She says that she loves her mother just the way she is, and she considers herself blessed, Jana expressed that if she ever had any daughters, she would teach them to be strong and independent.

Sissy

Sissy was the one and only child. She de-scribes having an amazing childhood.

Sissy says that she had so much love and was spoiled rotten! She said, "I had my mommy's heart and my daddy wrapped around my finger!"

Sissy stated that she was very close to her parents/mother, and since she was an only child, she didn't have to share with any other siblings. She exclaimed, "All the love was mine! They tried for a while to have me, so I was a blessing to them, and they adored me."

Sissy said that her mother was her best friend. "I could talk to her about anything. It didn't matter what it was, sex, bullies, drugs, friends, anything! She loved hard and I felt that. No matter what was said, or what argument, I was her one and only baby.

"I loved how much she loved me, but I will always remember from when I was a little girl, the ugly things she would say and do to me. She didn't know how to talk to me when I was a child. I remember once in the 5th grade; Mom drove me to school and she told me how fat I was. Instead of telling me in a motherly way she was very ugly to me, I remember crying in class because she was so hateful that morning. In the 7th grade, Mom did it again. On the way to school, she told me how fat and ugly I was and that no decent boy would ever want me! She slapped my glasses off of my face when I started crying.

"I started getting into boys so I could hurry up and move out, or prove to Mom that I had boyfriends, and that guys did like me. Sure, I was a little rebellious, and I had a mouth, but I never got in trouble with drugs, didn't have a baby until I was married, and she never got a call about her daughter being in trouble or jail. Things could have been much worse. I feel like I turned out just fine. I just wish she was here for me to ask her.

"I had plenty of love, talks, and under-standing, but I just wish she hadn't been so bipolar. She had all those mood swings, and she hurt my heart so much, making me wonder why I was such a horrible person. I guess now that she is gone, I will still never understand, or have clarity. The only thing I know is no matter what, she did love me!

"My mom taught me how to be a loving mother. She would have adored her grand-babies. She wanted them for so long, but once I had kids, she was so sick that she soon passed away. Mom didn't get to enjoy them, and she didn't get to see me, her baby girl, be a mommy.

"Mom taught me how to cook, and how to be with who is in my home and everyone else. She loved spending time with me and my dad. Mom was so happy and content not having a cell phone, and not watching TV. She just made memories, and taught me that making memories is priceless! We loved with all of our hearts and we were silly, and we enjoyed the little things. We had our ups and downs, but she was my only mom and I was her only baby!"

Sissy's mother became ill and passed away. She did get to meet a grandson, though, before she passed.

Alma

Alma explains that she was the baby of three girls. Her two older sisters were married and each had a child of their own. Alma's mother was strict and not affection-ate. Her father complied with whatever her mother wanted. He was a truck driver! The truth is that Alma's mother was verbally, emotionally, and physically abusive!

Alma displayed scars on her face and legs from her mother and on occasion, her father who had also beaten her. Alma explained that her mother ordered her father to beat her on her legs and Alma never knew why that beating occurred. The beatings, the slaps on the face, objects being thrown at her and being hit on her head or back, along with verbal and emotional abuse continued until she joined the Army after high school.

Alma had a job in retail. She recalled how her mother took all of her checks, minus $20, that Alma had to spend wisely for a whole month, to eat with and feed her two nephews that she babysat on her days off with no pay.

Every once in a while, Alma's mother allowed her to take the car to work. On this particular morning, after the usual slap on the face and belittlement, Alma goes to work, cashes her check, and buys hamburgers and beverages for her mother, father, and two nephews with her own $20 that was her budget for the month.

Alma states, "I guess Mama thought that I took too long because I was ten minutes late." When Alma opened the front door, she felt a sharp pain on her face from her nose to the top of her mouth. Her mother had turned four of her rings with the stones sticking out and struck her really hard on her face, nose, and gums. Alma remembers she almost fainted and could not stop bleeding. Alma recalled she was bleeding from everywhere.

The burgers rolled out of the sack and her father caught the drinks.

As she is telling her story, she is crying and I am also tearing up. Are you wondering if her mama apologized? No, she didn't.

She finally got her face to stop bleeding, and everybody else had already eaten. The next day Alma was forced by her mother to call in sick from work. The following day, with her face bruised and swollen, Alma got ready for work and was not allowed to take the car, so she ran to the bus stop that was quite a distance from her home. Having been told at the last minute that she could not take the car, she arrived late, disheveled, and with a swollen, bruised face.

Alma remembers her boss's face when he set his eyes on her. She said it was beet red. The boss asked her if her boyfriend had beat her, and Alma told him that she didn't have a boyfriend. He then asked her, "Who did it then?" Alma informed her boss that her Mama beat her because she had come home ten minutes late the day before yesterday.

Alma's boss explained to her that he couldn't allow her to work out on the floor with her face looking so bad. For that, afraid that her mother would beat her more, the boss allowed Alma to work in the back hanging up clothes. and told her "You have to get away from your mother."

During lunch, Alma recalls how hungry she was and was just sitting in the food court and the lady from one of the booths approached her and asked her if she would like a sandwich, fries, and a beverage. Alma responded, "No thank you, I'm not really hungry."

According to Alma, the kind lady explained to her that she had over-prepared too much food and would like for Alma to have some. Alma said that she ate well that day, and the kind lady confessed to Alma that she came from an abusive lifestyle her-self. So, Alma shared her story with the kind lady and they became instant friends. Alma recalls the soft-hearted lady saying, "You're being abused, leave."

That very same day, Alma walked around the mall and saw military recruiting offices and something clicked. Alma went by the naval office first, and there was no one there. So, she walked into the Marine office and the person sitting at the desk didn't appear interested in her.

She then went inside the Army office and was greeted by a friendly recruiter who asked her to sit down and talk. He was explaining how the Army was, and about being in the military. Alma asked questions and was very comfortable speaking with the recruiter. Alma told the recruiter that she was interested in joining. The recruiter asked her what happened to her face and if she was running away from something or someone.

Alma replied, "My mama beats me and I'm afraid she's going to kill me. My father allows the abuse and I want to join the Army,"

The recruiter told Alma, "You have to get away from your mother!"

Three people have already told me to get away from my mother, and I saw it as a sign from God."

Plans were made that day and Alma went home and announced to her family that she was joining the Army. Her mama told her "Good riddance!"

Alma gave her two-week notice to her boss and let him know that she was joining the Army! She also told her boss he could give her mama her last check! Alma recalls her boss saying that he would do no such thing and calmly said that "I will send it to you when you get where you are going." Alma said her mother never showed her face around her former place of employment.

Alma loved the military so much that she made it her career. She became a Major, and she met the love of her life in the military and they were married. Alma did go on a few visits home with her husband who was white. Alma is African-American.

She remembers her mama calling her names like "honky lover." Her mama would yell at her sisters, "Get that Nigger out of my house!"

The visits continued every now and then. Alma's mama would always pick up where she left off with her slurs and verbal abuse. Alma and her husband had three children, and Alma was quick to add, "I never had slapped them, or treated my children meanly."

Alma retired from the military and is now an administrator in a hospital. Recently her mama passed away. Alma got to see her and asked her "Mama, are you right?" Her mama just stared at her so she repeated, "Mama, are you right?" Alma said that her mom responded, "I know what you mean, am I right with God? Yes, I am right with God." Alma said her mama also told her "I'm sorry for everything and the way I treated you." Alma replied, "That's ok Mama. I forgave you a long time ago." Alma and her daughter are close and have a wonderful healthy relationship.

Veronica

Veronica was the second born in the family.

She has a brother who is two years older than she is. Veronica said that her mother worked two or three jobs, so her grandmother assisted with taking care of Veronica and her brother. Growing up was fast and furious for Veronica and she felt like she had to grow up quickly.

Her mother didn't have the time to form a mother/daughter bond according to Veronica. Veronica recalled how she had bonded with her father instead. While her brother was bonding with her mother, Veronica was becoming closest to her dad. Her brother loved being indoors with their mother. He loved cooking, and not getting his hands dirty. Veronica was more of a tomboy and loved sports. Her brother was a scholar and enjoyed school and making good grades. Veronica, on the other hand, says she loved being outdoors, working on her dad's car with him. She said she learned a lot and to this day she can assess what is going on with her car!

When Veronica was a teenager, she began to rebel and she says that she was craving attention. So she announced to her family that she was gay. She wasn't, but thought she would get their attention, one way or another! The parents threw her out of the house and she went and lived with relatives.

Veronica was allowed to return home and continued to rebel to get her mother's attention. When she was fifteen years old, she met a young man who was seventeen years old. He was smart in school and was about to graduate valedictorian when his parents were killed in a car accident. The young man quit school and later obtained a GED.

Veronica and he broke up due to his anger issues, and hers as well. Her mother didn't approve of her boyfriend and was happy to hear of the breakup.

Veronica received a call from him after a year had gone by, informing her that he had a baby son and that his ex-girlfriend had given up all rights to the baby and he needed her help!

Once again, Victoria left home and moved in with her boyfriend, but continued to attend school and sports. She recalled how they didn't have a clue on how to raise a baby, but she had babysat her cousins, so she used the skills that she had acquired. The boyfriend worked as a welder and was favored by his supervisors and sent to welding school.

Veronica said there were times when they had little money and would purchase a dollar hamburger and split it in half. The baby always had his formula, though.

During the day, Veronica and the boyfriend hired a relative of the boyfriend to babysit the baby. Veronica's parents were not on board with her taking on the responsibility of motherhood at sixteen years old!

Little or no contact took place between Veronica and her parents, and she did not ask for any kind of assistance, and they did not offer it either.

Veronica stated that her boyfriend began to be verbally and physically abusive toward her. According to her, she didn't just sit around and take it, though. Veronica would fight back also. She continued to attend school, play sports, and even had a scout talk to her about playing for them when she graduated!

Veronica happily shared her excitement with her mother and father, and they were truly ecstatic. She longed to have their approval for something! Veronica and her mother have grown closer through the years and enjoy their time together.

Angela

"My grandmother died the day after she gave birth to my mother." Angela said her mother was raised by relatives who apparently neglected her and saw her as a burden and deprived her of affection and nutrition. Often times her mother was left with a couple of male custodians, and Angela suspects that may have emotionally, verbally, and sexually abused her.

Angela describes her mother as growing up promiscuous. She had married Angela's father after she became pregnant with Angela, and then with her sister. They were seventeen months apart. Her parents eventually got divorced and her mother celebrated by buying alcohol.

Meanwhile, Angela's mother was drinking heavily and could not hold down a job.

She did manage to get a babysitting job for a short time. That is until she became so intoxicated that she was "falling down drunk," and according to Angela, she forgot all about the baby she was supposed to be taking care of. Angela was in grade school and recalls how the baby had not been fed or changed all day!

Angela's mother married a man in the military and he died in a plane crash. Angela described the marriage as very volatile.

Angela's biological father was in her life and she was able to see him and spend time with him and her stepmother, who was also an alcoholic.

Angela was in her teen years and re-members always fighting with her mother.

According to her, she was pretty much left to her own devices. Angela liked school and made good grades.

Angela babysat regularly and managed to buy groceries, buy clothes for her and her sister, and pay the bills. She continued to attend school, work, was in athletics, and pretty much was the head of the household.

Angela added that her mother continued going through "drinking binges." "Sometimes mom would pass out for three days!" Angela remembers throwing out her mother's bottles of vodka.

Angela's mother had one conversation with her about the "birds and the bees," and it wasn't the talk that Angela expected! Her mother drank the entire time and was being vulgar, telling Angela that she had better not "F***!" Needless to say, Angela was disgusted!

Angela's mother continued her drinking binges, and they continued to fight.

Meanwhile, Angela continued to go to school, work, and support her mother and sister.

Angela's father continued to be involved in her life and remained married to her stepmother, who continued to also consume alcohol excessively, but realized Angela and her mother needed extensive counseling and her mother required to detox.

Angela's mom was smoking up to three packs of cigarettes a day. She had also participated in a rehabilitation program, was diagnosed with cancer of the palate, bone cancer, and eventually passed away due to having a stroke.

Angela has a grown daughter, has a good relationship with her, and is respectful of her decisions, and life.

Angela remembered visiting her mother in the hospital before she passed away.

She vividly recalls taking her mom a rose and her mother saying "I love you" repeatedly.

Ginger

"I grew up with my grandmother. My Mama gave me up when I was eleven months old. She was in and out of my life." Ginger said she hated her mom for many years. Every time Ginger would try and ask her mother why, it was to no avail and her mother would refuse to speak about it. Ginger described her mother as a "restless spirit." Ginger's grandmother, with the help of her aunts, raised Ginger well and she was con-tent and had a happy childhood, except for her mom coming and going from her life.

When Ginger's grandmother passed away, Ginger went to live with her mother in another state. Her mother had married and she had a stepfather. Ginger did not go into detail, but the stepfather was a bad per-son. It was so bad that on graduation day, Ginger bought a bus ticket and left.

Several years later, her mother came back into her life. By this time, Ginger had children of her own and was divorced.

Ginger had been working on herself and said, "I wasn't really religious, but I was spiritual," Her pastor had been talking with her about "forgiveness." Ginger decided to forgive her mother.

One day her mother, who had been living with Ginger, became very ill, and Ginger made a promise that if the good Lord let her mother live, she would forgive her mother, and herself for all the anger and hatred she had ever felt in her heart. The Lord spared her mother and they did form a mother/daughter kind of relationship.

Ginger's mother left again after a day of recuperating after a lengthy hospital stay.

Ginger explained that she was at work when her daughter called and said, "Mama, Grandma done gone and left us!"

Ginger's mom had rented an apartment and preferred being by herself. Ginger accepted her mother the way she was and her mother accepted her the way that she was, and they got along and respected one another just the way they were! Ginger's mother passed away soon after, and Ginger was glad they had formed a good relation-ship.

Ginger raised her two daughters on her own with little help from her ex-husband. The girls were different in personality and attitude, said Ginger. The oldest was quiet and soft-spoken, but if the need arose, she could stand up strong! The second child was vocal and outspoken.

Ginger expressed having a different relationship with each one. The second child would tell others that Ginger loved the first daughter better than her. Ginger said, "You love all your children the same, just in different ways!"

The girls grew up and had children of their own. "One beautiful, soft-spoken, funny, and strong, the second, beautiful, outspoken, and restless like my mother," Ginger said.

One day, Ginger went to the second daughter's place of employment and her beautiful daughter and she made small talk. As Ginger was walking away, her daughter said, "Mom, I love you!" To which Ginger replied, "I love you too!"

Ginger describes that she felt something then as she was walking away, but she brushed it off. As Ginger was nearing the door she felt something telling her to turn around, and her daughter had walked half-way behind Ginger to watch her walk away.

The following day, Ginger did not receive her usual call from her precious daughter, so she took it upon herself to go to her place of employment, only to be told that her daughter had clocked out and gone home. Ginger quickly went to her daughter's home just in time to hold her precious daughter one more time and to hear her take her last breath. Ginger's precious daughter had taken her own life.

Ginger stated, "I'm not angry, I just don't know why she did it. It just still drives me crazy."

Ginger was nothing like her mother.

Ginger tried to teach her daughters to be strong, kind, and forgiving. Her one remaining daughter is all of the above!

Lori

Lori was the second-born child. Her mother was not affectionate, as Lori explained how her mother and aunt had been raised by her grandfather and he always left them alone to fend for themselves.

Lori's parents were married, had a son, and then Lori was born. Apparently, Lori's mother almost died giving birth to her and used it against Lori verbally and emotion-ally.

Lori was close to her father. Her father was present whenever her mother would scream at Lori that everything was her fault. Lori's father would not defend her.

Lori recalled one day she was picked up by her mother from school and asked to see her report card. According to Lori, her mother was not pleased and took Lori to the cemetery alone, and later picked her up!

Lori stated, "I was only six years old!" Her mother would make her feel like she was unwanted and useless.

On another occasion, Lori dropped the meatloaf, glass plate, and all, and the mother berated her saying, "I hope you bleed to death!" Apparently, Lori had cut herself picking up the pieces. She had stepped on the broken glass, causing her to be taken to the ER!

Lori's father passed away and she lost the only person who had treated her nicely.

Lori's mother continued her emotional and verbal abuse. When Lori was seventeen, she began to go out but was not allowed if her mother was in a bad mood. According to Lori,

"She was in a bad mood all the time!" It became so bad that her mother made her place her hand on the Bible and swear that she would not be going out.

Lori married, gave birth to her daughter, and was very quickly divorced, so she went back to live with her mother.

"She was a terrible grandmother to my daughter." Then her mother would tell the granddaughter that she didn't mean to be cruel. Lori needed assistance with the care of her mother but she refused.

On another occasion, the mother threw a temper tantrum and went into Lori's room and destroyed it! She destroyed her jewelry, cut up Lori's clothes, and summoned the neighbor to witness the destruction she had created and told the neighbor, "She hurts me!" Lori remembers the look of disgust and disbelief on the neighbor's face!

After the neighbor left, her mother screamed "This house is mine!"

Lori stated her mother was nice and civil to others. Lori was bullied by her mother and was reminded that she was to stay home, not go out, and that no men were allowed in the home. Lori described life with her mother as unbearable and she had to put up with the abuse because she had nowhere else to go and was unemployed. Lori had one female friend that would come over when her mother was asleep, and they would talk outside.

The mother was very obese and ordered Lori to wait on her "hand and foot." But as her mother became more and more obese, she had other health issues and made Lori promise she would never place her-in a nursing home. Lori kept her promise and took good care of her mother till the day she passed away.

Lori said her daughter is her one bright spot and she realizes her mother was a bitter, narcissistic woman and loved Lori in her own way. Lori expressed that she will definitely teach her daughter not to ever allow anyone to bully her, or disrespect her in any way.

Mary Linda

Mary Linda was the third to the oldest of seven children. She was small for her age so her mother made sure Mary Linda got extra fruit to eat. With seven children, there were times when Mary Linda would be playing outside and her siblings would eat their part plus hers!

Her mother would go to the supermarket for groceries and buy extra fruit, and hide it for Mary Linda. The older sister soon discovered the secret and would take the extra fruit so Mary Linda didn't get any! When Mary Linda's sister confronted their mother, she explained that Mary Linda was small and she was worried about her not eating right.

Things became a little better after that!

Mary Linda's mother had been married prior to her marriage to her children's father. Her mother had been in love with her first husband and told Mary Linda all about their love stories and how much in love they had been! Mary Linda recalls the look on her mother's face when she reminisced about the gifts, trips, and dancing that they had shared! Every payday, the first husband would "surprise" her with a new dress. They never had children and had been married for only a few years when he passed away.

A few years later, Mary Linda's mother met her second husband. He had been in the military and liked to drink and womanize. There had not been time for vacations or family time with seven children.

Mary Linda does not recall any affection between her parents, or toward her and her siblings. It was understood that they were loved, cared for, and had a roof over their heads. The four girls grew up and formed a good sibling bond with each other.

The oldest married young and years later, Mary Linda married. It appeared that the remaining three were wanting to escape the strict environment and begin their own lives.

Mary Linda recalls how her mother wanted the best for her and her siblings. Mary Linda remembers the day she shared the news with her mother about getting married.

Mary Linda said her mother was over-joyed and then began to give her "the talk." Mary Linda recalls her mother telling her that men were men, and that as long as they worked and were good providers, she was to just turn her head to any indiscretions, or gossip. Mary Linda followed her mother's advice and put up with her first husband for several years before divorcing him and having to work before and after the divorce.

During the marriage, a daughter was born and there was little to no support from Mary Linda's husband.

Mary Linda met another man who bought her gifts and furs, took her on trips, and frequented expensive restaurants. Life appeared good to others, but it wasn't so. This husband was possessive, degrading, and a womanizer. He enjoyed parading her around like a trophy. He ended up leaving Mary Linda for another woman.

Mary Linda met and married another man. He had the same personality and mindset as the other two and they ultimately divorced.

Her daughter grew up and let Mary Linda know that she would marry and be equal to her husband. She would not put up with any indiscretions, shenanigans, verbal, emotional, or any other kind of abuse. She would not, under any circumstances, turn her face to any wrongdoing by any man.

Mary Linda and her mother remained close and she never told her mother how her advice had not been conducive to a good marriage. Mary Linda is happy being single and is supportive of her daughter's lifestyle and decisions. They continue to respect one another and are as close as two peas in a pod!

Marie

Marie was the firstborn to her young mother. Marie said, "I was a c-section baby and my mother never bonded with me!" Marie said right away that mother had postpartum depression, as well as bipolar depression. She had also separated from Marie's father before she was born.

Marie's grandparents became aware of the situation and took Marie home with them from the hospital! The grandparents were supposed to return baby Marie to her mother in three days, so they took off to the little town where Marie's mother resided at the time. The grandparents got caught in a flood and had to turn back.

Her mother didn't inquire about Marie so the grandparents raised her. Marie stated that she didn't see her mother again until she was grown. She explained how she attempted to get close to her mother, but it was to no avail. They were like stranger and there was no mother/daughter relationship!

Her grandparents were her mother and father.

"My great-grandmother was from an Indian reservation, and had twenty-one children! My grandmother was one of them. Someone had even written an article about my family history."

My grandfather passed away and my grandmother never remarried." Marie said that her grandmother lived to be 84 years old. She learned a lot from her grandmother and how she kept traditions. She was the glue of the family,

Marie's mother had other children.

Marie is not close to her half-siblings and has not spoken to her mother in two years.

She is content with her present life!

Mari

Mari was the middle of five siblings. She said that her growing-up years were "great." Mari stated that her mother was a very respectable and beautiful woman. She ad-mitted her mother and she didn't see eye to eye at times, but added that her mother knew she was "that daughter who would do anything for her."

Mari said the holidays were filled with amazing food, "simple and amazing!" She said the menu consisted of beans with everything! Fideos, tortillas, carne guisada, enchiladas, tacos and chicken.

Other family favorites were casserole papas (potatoes) with meat and carnitas (small pieces of meat) pasta with meat and rice, everything served with beans!

Mari said that besides her mother being respectable, she was also loving, and made Mari and her siblings feel loved and safe. "I think she loved my sister more!" Mari said she always felt that way. "There is nothing I would have changed about my mother. I loved her just the way she was!"

Mari said that she has one daughter and they are very close. Mari said she learned respect from her mother, and like her mother, she has taught her daughter to be respectful to herself and others.

Natalia

Natalia was the fourth of eight children. Her mother was a single mother and worked hard at being a good provider.

The first two oldest daughters babysat the other siblings, and when Natalia quit school in the fourth grade, she was in charge of her younger siblings. Natalia had quit school due to a teacher hitting her on the back with a ruler, cutting her back.

One of the oldest girls got married. The next oldest sibling made pastries, ironed and sewed for others in order to be able to help with groceries, and ultimately, for the purchase of their home, which turned out to be a hoax. It appeared that the man who "sold" Natalia's mother the home had lied to her and did not have any real intention of allowing her to own the house. It was some-thing that Natalia's mother never got over.

Natalia's brothers also worked outside the home doing odd jobs. Natalia babysat and entertained her younger siblings. The last sibling just happened to be a green-eyed, red-headed baby girl. Natalia also helped to raise her other two younger sisters as well. She remembers holding her doll in one arm and her baby sister in the other arm. When the other two female siblings would run off, Natalia would place her baby sister on a blanket on the bare ground and chase the other two curious girls! As the years went by, Natalia began to work, cleaning houses and polishing silver.

When Natalia was sixteen years of age, her mother died of cancer. Before the mother died, she asked that the family remain close. The family remained close and Natalia raised her siblings the best that she could.

Natalia learned how to cook delicious meals and kept the traditions of her mother and passed those traditions to her daughters. Natalia taught her daughters to be ladies and to be kind and honest, especially to themselves,

Having been orphaned at such a young age, Natalia had lost so much of her child-hood. Ultimately, she had three boys and three girls. Natalia was more lenient with the boys than with the girls. She explained that they were her mother's teachings. Natalia taught her daughters that if they went down the wrong path, or became pregnant if the boy didn't marry them, they would not be able to do all the things they had wanted to do, plus they were going to be stuck with a baby to raise alone! The boys, on the other hand, could start all over again like nothing ever happened.

Natalia knew her daughters did not agree with her allowing the sons to get away with so much, and not having many rules like the daughters were supposed to abide by.

Natalia admitted that time had changed her so much and she realized how hard she had been on her daughters but added that they thank her for a lot of things she taught them. "The rest was up to them, to take or leave what they were taught,"

Natalia said that she was against the daughters wanting to go out with girl-friends to clubs, join organizations, or go on girls' trips while they were married. Natalia said that marriages were hard enough without the wife being out of the home and being involved in extracurricular activities.

She described her daughters as friendly, popular, and very outgoing. Her daughters Natalia knew her daughters did not agree with her allowing the sons to get away with so much, and not having many rules like the daughters were supposed to abide by.

Natalia admitted that time had changed her so much and she realized how hard she had been on her daughters but added that they thank her for a lot of things she taught them. "The rest was up to them, to take or leave what they were taught,"

Natalia said that she was against the daughters wanting to go out with girl-friends to clubs, join organizations, or go on girls' trips while they were married. Natalia said that marriages were hard enough without the wife being out of the home and being involved in extracurricular activities.

She described her daughters as friendly, popular, and very outgoing. Her daughters were offended when Natalia expressed her concern.

Natalia was a housewife and a stay-at-home mom. Her husband worked hard to make a decent living. Natalia admitted that she admired her daughters for wanting to be more than just wives and mothers. She knew they wouldn't allow any man to take advantage of them or abuse them. Natalia recalled an incident that occurred the week after she and her husband were married. Natalia stated she considers herself a good cook; after all, she had utilized her cooking skills on her seven siblings. Natalia had prepared something special for their newlywed meal. After the meal, Natalia asked her husband if he had liked it, when out of his mouth came the response, "It didn't taste like my mother's food. I'm so used to different tasting food!" Natalia said that was most definitely the wrong answer, so she very calmly sat down in front of her husband and said, "If you miss your mama's food that much, then go back home, it's not too late!" She added, "That solved that!"

Natalia said that two of her daughters were good cooks and that one couldn't even boil water! She said that she taught her sons and daughters not to "sweat the small stuff in life, because it's just not worth it. It's just peanuts!"

Susie

Susie said that she was the oldest of four brothers and two sisters. Susie laughs and explained how she thought she would be an only child, but the sisters and brothers came along.

Her father was a hard worker and held two jobs. Susie's mother worked at home, cooking, cleaning, and raising six children.

Susie babysat her siblings at an early age. She recalls not being close to her mother as she was strict with Susie as she was growing up. Susie was not allowed to spend the night at anyone's house, but a friend could spend the night with her. As a teenager, she resented not being able to "hang out" with her friends as much as she wanted.

Susie and her mother didn't have the time for mother/daughter talks. She was expected to go to school, make good grades and help with the younger children,

Susie was allowed to go on dates and dances as she became a junior, and then a senior in high school. Many of Susie's female friends were married while they were still in high school. She attended her Junior and Senior Proms, and her mother made sure Susie looked and felt like a princess.

Susie said that both her mother and father were proud of her when she graduated.

She realized she did not want to get married and wanted more out of her life,

Susie stated she knew she did not want any children either, especially because she had to help with five other siblings!

Susie went off to college became a nurse, and much later married and had two daughters. She also became closer to her mother and had great talks about mother-hood and husbands!

Susie claims she is nontraditional and made her own traditions with her family and taught her daughters to be strong. She also made the realization that perhaps she could have tried earlier on to talk with her mother about things.

They grew closer through the years and Susie was home when her mother passed away. Susie has fond memories of her mother.

Leeza

Leeza was the only child in her family, and her mother provided for her as best as she could. According to Leeza, her mother was a beautiful woman and Leeza admired her sense of style. Her mother, however, lacked self-esteem and self-confidence, according to Leeza. Leeza loved her mother dearly but was an independent spirit and lived out on her own, with her mother's assistance.

Leeza made no mention of having any kind of relationship with her biological father. Her mother did not maintain healthy relationships. She married a man who was abusive verbally as well as physically. Leeza stated that her mother always had some kind of excuse for her stepfather, and apologized for his abusive behavior.

Leeza visited her mother in the state that she lived in and stayed for three weeks.

Leeza said that her stepfather was a bad man and she had a bad feeling about him. Her mother continued to make excuses for him, and he continued to be abusive.

Leeza informed her stepfather was arrested for stealing from the business where he worked, and was confronted by the owners and fired. He went home and shot Leeza's mother in the head. Leeza remembers the phone call informing her that her mother had been murdered. Her stepfather denied any involvement in the homicide. Leeza wanted a funeral for her beautiful mother, but her stepfather had her cremated. She was devastated and said, "I had no say so!"

It wasn't long before it was discovered that her stepfather had been the one that had shot her mother. Leeza was there when her stepfather was in the process of being

arrested. He saw her standing outside, smirked, and said, "I shot your mother and you were next!" He then smirked again and shot himself in the head.

Leeza lost her grandparents and several friends that same year. She described feeling lost and depressed and was ready to give up!

Leeza soon began therapy and now rescues all kinds of animals. She loves her "mini zoo" and keeps it going via donations and food banks for her and her animals,

Leeza loves to dress beautifully like her mother. She is independent and self-confident, despite having some health issues. Speaking of health issues, Leeza's state is currently on complete lockdown and cur-few due to Covid-19. She is receiving grief therapy via phone, and her physicians are checking up on her. Leeza remains hopeful that she will not contract this horrible virus. Two of her doctors' nurses presently have Covid-19.

God bless you, Leeza, and God bless the world.

Arlena

Arlena was raised by a single mom. Her mother and father divorced, and Arlena had seven siblings, and five of her older siblings had married young. Arlena was left at home to take care of her two younger siblings, as her mother held down two jobs.

A few years later, Arlena's mother remarried another man that was not nice to her mother, her, or her other two siblings. Arlena's mother continued to work and her husband also worked but did not contribute to the household.

Arlena began seeing a young man and became pregnant. Her stepfather was mad and verbally aggressive, so Arlena moved out and lived with one of her older sisters. She finished school and had her beautiful daughter.

Arlena's mother did visit her once after she had her daughter and continued to re-side with the cold-hearted stepfather. After Arlena's daughter was ten years of age, she met her present husband, who treats her well and they work well together as a team. Together they are raising her daughter and have a five-year-old son of their own,

Her mother eventually had to stop working, and Arlena's stepfather was not happy. He actually believed that his wife was put under a spell and needed to be cured, in Mexico, where he was originally from, and where his relatives resided.

Without Arlena's or her siblings' knowledge, their stepfather did not allow their mother to notify them of her departure to Mexico. When Arlena and the family found out their mother was gone, they confronted their stepfather, who then admitted that he had left her in Mexico, to be cured, as he believed that she was under some form of a spell. Arlena was mortified!

She had been to Mexico when she was younger and she remembered where her stepfather's family resided. Along with two other family members, Arlena drove to Mexico and knocked on the door. She could see inside the living room through the screen door and she observed her mother sitting in a wooden chair with no cushion or pillow, and she was facing the wall!

When her mother heard Arlena's voice, she used all her strength to get up and grab Arlena by the arm and said, "Let's go!"

Arlena recalls how her mother and she became closer and she has taught her daughter to be kind, strong, and loving. Arlena stated that she will teach her daughter to stand up for herself and not to be submissive.

Beebee

"I don't know if I'm going to go see my mama for Mother's Day, or not, because I really don't like her! She did call me not too long ago and all I could hear was crying, so I handed the phone to my sister. My sister tried to get me to talk to my mother, but I didn't have anything to say!

"My grandmother brought me up, and I lived with her until she died. My mother had three children and my sister lived with one aunt and my brother lived with my grandmother and me.

"My mother was and still is on drugs. She had us at a young age but could not take care of us! Grandmother cared for my brother and me and tried to discourage my mother from her dangerous lifestyle, but it was to no avail!

"Grandmother worked and we had what we needed. She put a roof over our heads, ate well, and had clothes on our backs.

"I started working at seventeen years of age. I was able to help with groceries and buy my own clothes. My mother kept on doing drugs and coming and going into our lives."

Beebee remembers her mother leaving and knowing that she would not return, as she had issues in the city where she resided.

Beebee's grandmother became ill and suffered for a few years before she passed away. Beebee continued to live in the home and her aunt and friends came and went. She recalls overhearing family talking about her mother coming back to pick up the younger siblings. Beebee knew they didn't want to go live with a mother they really didn't know. Therefore, Beebee made the decision to rent and apartment, furnished it the best that they could, and she moved with her siblings to their new home, Beebe works hard, supports her siblings, sends them to school and encourages them to do well in school, and above all, loves them! Beebee added, "I definitely do not want to9 live the lifestyle of my mother."

Hortensia

Hortensia came from a large family. She was the third born of ten siblings. When Hortensia was ten and a half years old, her parents and the two older sisters, and the baby, immigrated to the US.

Hortensia was left behind to care for the younger siblings. Before her parents departed for the US, Hortensia's mother bought her a new dress, shoes, and socks. It was her first new dress ever! She had always worn hand-me-downs from her older sisters,

Later, she learned that the clothes were going-away presents!

Hortensia was left with her grandmother and step-grandfather. She was sexually abused by two of her uncles, and her step-grandfather verbally abused her. Once Hortensia's grandfather picked up a huge rock and threw it at her, bruising her arm and back, and she didn't know why.

They lived out on a farm and after Hortensia would get the younger siblings up for school, and prepared their breakfasts and lunches, she would get her chores done.

Hortensia's grandparents had twenty cows that needed to be milked daily, and this was her job.

Her mother would call and write letters, and her grand-mother would tell her what to say and what to write.

Hortensia's parents returned after being gone for eighteen months and right away had Hortensia assisting in a lab where she would stick fingers, write down the person's name, and walk them into the city.

Hortensia recalls having a lot of anger and resentment toward her parents, especially her mother. She said she felt abandoned, her emotions were out of control, and therefore she mistreated her mother.

Hortensia stated she had missed out on love, affection, or any kind of warmth from her mother. Hortensia realized that she did not have a normal childhood, because she had been robbed of her innocence. Her mother stayed busy working and Hortensia stayed busy being a mother to her siblings, Hortensia was depressed, tired, and sick with tonsillitis. It didn't matter; she was still expected to work. Her mother saw how ill Hortensia was and told her she could share her younger sister's antibiotics.

Hortensia said she was so sick and felt herself fading away and described having an "out-of-body experience." Hortensia could see herself staring at herself in a mirror. For the first time, her mother showed concern and offered her food. It was then that Hortensia had a change of heart and accepted her mother's first sign of warmth. Hortensia stated that was a defining moment for her. She began to see that her mother was trying to change. "I began to grow up into a young lady and all I wanted was to leave home and get married. I taught my younger siblings how to work the land. I met my husband-to-be, and he had to leave to work in another state. He asked for my hand via letter and for nine months

my mother was hesitant and would not respond. My fiancé finally came for me. We were married and had three children. I am different from my mother, just like the difference between the North and South! I show my daughters affection and we have a great, loving relationship with my husband. He calls us his queens!

"I do have a better relation-ship with my mother now.

Every time we talk she asks for forgiveness, and I keep telling her that I forgive her and I ask her to forget the past because I have."

Hortensia said she is very spiritual and reads the Bible. She shared how fulfilling it is to hear "The Word" with her mother. Her mother also reads the Bible. Hortensia stated, "We're mother and daughter now!"

Juanita #1

Juanita was the oldest of seven children, her parents were farmers and worked in the fields. Juanita and her siblings were all born at home via a midwife. The children all attended a country school until they consolidated to town. Juanita recalls her mother was very loving and they had a great relationship. "I could tell Mother anything!"

Juanita recalled being three years old and knocking her father out with a large stick! Her mother scolded her but when her father regained consciousness, he said it was ok!

"We would go to Mother for everything before we went to Daddy.

"Two of my older sisters died young. One had married young, had a baby, and died!" Her brothers also died, and one was a brittle diabetic, Juanita said.

"Mother taught us to cook, sew, and we all had chores to complete. We made our clothes on a throttle sewing machine and washed clothes on a rub board!"

We cooked on an old wooden stove, and we also had a wooden ice box. The ice man came around every other day. Mother allowed us to go to the country store to buy candy. She made sure we attended church on Sunday,

Juanita's mother had a way of manipulating her father and making him think it was his idea!

The holidays were special Juanita recalls. She described the meal as consisting of baked hen, dressing, and canned green beans. Juanita said that they had a garden and they canned fruit and vegetables in the summer to have plenty for the winter!

As Juanita was growing up her mother would not talk with her or her sister (who by the way was the baby and was plain rotten!) about the opposite sex or relationships.

Juanita described these kinds of talk as "taboo!"

Juanita was working in a restaurant as a waitress and noticed a good-looking cowboy coming in to eat at the restaurant every day. He finally got the courage to ask her out! Juanita said they would go to church, to the movies, and on long walks. They dated for a year and Juanita's cowboy asked her father for her hand in marriage and he approved. They bought furniture and rented a house before they were married. They had two boys and two girls. Juanita's beautiful mother died of a blood clot, as she had an enlarged heart. Her sweet father died from stomach cancer. Juanita's handsome cowboy husband also died of cancer. Juanita recalled how rough and sad it was during her husband's hospitalization and passing away there. Juanita said she had a stroke prior to her husband's illness and wasn't feeling well herself. The love for her husband pulled her through.

When life starts getting hard, Juanita's favorite saying is "My nose is running and my feet are smelling!"

Juanita's advice to her daughters is "Follow your heart and trust God because without him you cannot make it!" She has advice for her sons also. She told them, "Treat girls like you would want your sisters to be treated!"

Juanita #2

Juanita said that she was the youngest of three siblings She described being and feeling loved, and was overprotected by her parents. Juanita said that her siblings teased her "endlessly." Juanita said she was a crybaby.

"I was very close to my mother, especially in the later years when my dad passed away and we moved in together. Prior to that, I was a daddy's girl. My mom always wanted the best for me and I felt the love, but she always scared my friends because she was very strict.

"My dad was the total opposite. Very kind, generous, and could not say no to me. My mom was beautiful inside and out. She always dressed up nicely, cooked the best food, and always encouraged all of us to do our best. She had become a mom at age nine when her mother passed away and she had to take over the household and the raising of the younger siblings.

"She then married and had four children of her own and made us all feel special and over-protected. I loved her very much but her only fault was that she was too strict and too overly protective. She never allowed me to go to friends' houses, never allowed sleepovers. I was not allowed to walk home with my friends or meet my friends at the movies. We were not allowed to go swimming because we might drown. Mom did have different rules for my brother. He was allowed to do all those things because he was a boy.

"We don't have the same traditions or habits. Mom was happily married for over fifty years and raised three girls and one boy as a stay-at-home mom, She did not have the luxury of formal education but had many talents. She was a leader, disciplinarian, a good and loyal wife.

"Relatives always made their first stop at my mom's house for a good meal and cheerful conversation. I, on the other hand, married and divorced, raised two sons on my own, and had the opportunity for a good education and employment.

"I don't have the cooking skills and hospitality and traditions that my mom did. "I miss the Thanksgiving, Christmas, Lent, and Easter traditions. I do find myself being spiritual like she was. She instilled her faith in us. I miss so many things about my mom. Her beautiful smile, her prayerful self, blessing everyone, her funny jokes, and her strength through good times and bad. She definitely left a lasting legacy.

Juanita #3

Juanita is the middle child of three siblings. She said she grew up centered around extended family, a whole city block!

"My grandparents lived on one side, uncles and aunts beside them, and we lived at the other end. My paternal great grandparents live down the street with extended relatives on 2-3 blocks around them.

My maternal grandparents lived on a farm close by and we visited nearly every weekend until we moved when I was in the second grade. We moved four times until I was in the seventh grade. We stayed in Big Spring.

"My dad was a very hard worker and both he and my mom knew the value of family ties and history. We often traveled to South Texas where both of my parents were born, and also to places like Guadalajara and Mexico City where I attended a soccer game during the Olympics!

"Religion also ranked top priority in our family, If I went to my grandmother's house in the late afternoon, I knew I'd have to stay to pray the Rosary with my aunts and uncles and any other cousins there." My family always helped at Jamaicas and as kids, we attended CCD and the CYD.

"I mostly spent my growing up around cousins, especially those who like dancing. We would go to dances as an extended family with our parents, uncles, aunts, and cousins.

"My mom insisted on us get-ting a strong education. She did not hesitate to speak up for her rights or others' rights;

however, if we were in the wrong, she never used the "chancla" but did use the belt, twigs, or her hand! Plus, I learned about good money habits such as waiting for "sales" from my mom. Now at 95, she continues being that strong-willed viejita!

"We have always been close, and I admire my mom's resilience! She would make my dad be the one to tell us what we should do or not do, though I knew many times it was her feelings and not his!"

Juanita said that she shares her mom's love of family, religion, culture, and love of gardening. She admits she is more like her father. Juanita has a daughter and feels she has taught her the love of family, the importance of faith and culture, plus independence.

"My mom continues to have a strong spirit and our relationship has somewhat changed due to her age which is common among aging parents.

"We continue to go out and eat, and shopping together when her health is good and when she's in the mood. She can beat me on any day on a shopping spree if she's having a good day and not getting tired until she gets home! My mom's memory of people is far better than mine! I'm a ghost when it comes to her grandchildren and her great-grandchildren, LOL! It's great though to see her loving on them through hugs, tenderness, and always asking about how they are doing.

Luce

Luce was an only child until she was 24 years old and married. "At that time, my parents adopted my sister who was a year and ten months old. My mother was 52 years old when they adopted my sister.

"While growing up, my house was very quiet and calm, my parents doted on me, and bought me anything I wanted within reason, except for a pony. I was a very responsible child, and even though I was spoiled, I knew the worth of a dollar, and I even started working at the age of 15.

"My parents and I were very close. I was a big Daddy's girl and my mom doted on me, and even though we had a large extended family, it was us three against the world. We protected each other, we defended each other, and our family always came first. There was nothing I couldn't talk to my parents about.

"My mom was very proper, but her family came first, and she kept a spotless home. You could always smell the Pine Sol on Saturday mornings. I remember waking up to Tejano music, the smell of Pine Sol, and tortillas cooking.

"Mom was very much the underdog of her siblings. Therefore, my dad was very protective of her. My friends loved her. She has always been so outgoing and will give you the shirt off her back. She raised my sister and helped her raise her four children. She has a wonderful sense of humor and loves everyone, always finds the good in others. She is one of the kindest people I know.

"She seemed to be very strong and ready to help any-one. Everyone loves my mom, no matter where we go; she's the belle of the ball, takes forever to get out of Wal-Mart because of all the people who want to greet her. My mom is exactly what I would have chosen as a mom. I would not change a thing about her.

"My mom has taught me to be strong, hard-working, and independent. She could be strict with curfews. My friends and I still tell horror stories about her coming after us if we were five minutes late. You had to be respectful and most importantly, have respect for yourself.

"I taught my sister to have self-respect, to work hard, to keep your word, to be depend-able and NEVER be dependent on a man! Oh, and to always pull your eyelid down, never out as it creates wrinkles. Also, you don't have to be perfect, just feel good about yourself, for you, and not for someone else, dress for you, go by your mirror, not anyone else's opinion. You can look sexy but still be ladylike.

"My mom is 93 years old and has dementia. 1 have become the mom most times; she is de-pendent on my sister and me, but I am her primary caretaker. We are still able to socialize together and clean the house and cook together. 1 treasure every day I have with her and cannot imagine my life without her. She can still be a lot of fun. She loves to go out to eat and enjoys a good margarita. This girl is my best friend."

Diann

Diann was the third child of six. She recalls how growing up was like a "roller coaster. Mom was married three times.

"We moved several times when she was married to her second husband in the military. He was abusive to his stepchildren (my older brother, sister, and me). He was sent to Vietnam and we ended up coming back to West Texas. It was a cultural shock, to say the least!

"After they divorced, Mom had to work two jobs to support five kids, so we were alone a lot. Our social life consisted of school and church,

"Also, after having grown up in nice homes and having nice clothes, our income dropped drastically and we lived a very poor life.

"Mom was a very good mother. She sacrificed a lot for us. I don't remember her ever spanking us. She had the patience of Job. She was a virtuous woman despite having been married three times.

"Mom's first two husbands left her for other women. She always presented and carried herself as a lady. She did the best she could in raising her children. Mom seemed to think that she needed a man to give her security. She didn't feel she could provide a good enough life for us. She was very submissive to her husbands. Her last husband was physically and mentally abusive to Mom, but she refused to leave him even though we begged her to. Mom took care of him until the day he died.

"I am very close to my mother now but it wasn't al-ways so. When she remarried the third time, she moved away. When I had my babies, she was not present, nor did she come to help me after the babies were home. By the time she had her last child, she really wasn't a grandmother to my children, and it hurt my feelings. It wasn't until she was diagnosed with Parkinson's disease that we became close.

"My mother taught me to be a social worker. She was always happy to help others even if it meant she did without. She doesn't have a mean bone in her body. She taught me to respect my elders. She taught me manners, and she taught me to love the Lord. The most important thing though, that she taught me was that I was a strong woman who had brains and didn't have to rely on a man to have worth. She taught me that I could do anything as long as I didn't give in or give up!

"I do keep holiday traditions such as Christmas. My mom's favorite holiday is Christmas.

Even now that she is in the nursing home, she has to have a Christmas tree in her room!"

Her mother's advice is to "Never give up on your dreams, so that they leave footprints for someone else to follow perhaps."

Rachel

Rachel was the fourth of five sisters. Growing up was fun and she said that they had a happy life.

Her mother was very soft-spoken and gentle. Her father was strict, but both parents were caring and loving,

Rachel's mother was a cook for the school and knew how to prepare delicious meals. Her father built the younger siblings a beautiful playhouse and they spent their time playing in it, as did the neighborhood girls!

Holidays were fun and special with family and friends, and of course, with all kinds of delicious food!

Rachel described her mother as mild-mannered and when she and her siblings were mis-behaving, she would tell them, "Wait till your dad gets home!" But most of the time, she didn't even tattle on them.

"My mom was religious and enjoyed helping at the church." Rachel said that she was very close to her mother. While her mother was at work, her two older sisters would look after the three younger sisters. All of the siblings and Rachel loved and respected their mother for teaching them how to be patient, and kind, and not to be judgmental because no one is perfect!

Rachel has all boys and has told them to be respectful and supportive to their wives, especially if they are employed.

"Their home is their castle too!"

"Be wise, be good, and always do the right thing!"

Rachel had four granddaughters and they get along great, and she has taught them to be loving and to be true to themselves.

Mary

Mary is the second to the oldest of five siblings. According to her, she didn't have the "typical upbringing." Mary describes being raised by old-fashioned parents with "olden Filipino ways."

It was understood that her mother and father loved them but there was no affection, physically or verbally.

Mary and her siblings were only a year apart and were close with each other and supportive and respectful as well.

The Christmas holidays were celebrated with delicious Filipino dishes.

Mary described her mother as being strict and stern, and a stay-at-home mom.

Mary stated that she and her siblings were not allowed to receive gifts from friends and remembers how her sister was given an inexpensive gift from a little female friend, and then how their mother forbade her to keep it and made her sister return it to her friend. The friend's mother wrote a note to Mary's mother explaining that the gift was a token of their friendship and that it was ok with her for her daughter to give it to Mary's sister. After that, Mary's sister was allowed to keep the gift.

Mary explained how her mother did the best she could to make ends meet, and taught Mary and her siblings to save what money they had and to be frugal.

When Mary went to college out of town, her mother would prepare a week's worth of meals to take to classes on a daily basis. She did not have the luxury to eat out. "I learned to prioritize from my mother."

Mary met a nice man and married. They had a daughter and decided to move to the U.S. with visas. Mary's daughter aged out and had to return to the Philippines where she is studying to be a physical therapist. "We are affectionate with each other."

Mary said that her daughter will hopefully return to the states to work.

She describes their relation-ship as good. Her daughter is "too trusting!" According to Mary, she had to teach her daughter to be "street smart and sensible." "I have to trust her." Mary said that she has instilled morals, values, and respect.

Teresa

Teresa was the fourth of six siblings. She informed her oldest brother died in a tragic car accident in a small town where they lived in Texas. The family later moved to another small town, but it was still larger than the previous town that they had lived in.

Teresa's mom was not affectionate and never told them that she loved them. "We just felt it in our hearts." Teresa said that it hurt not to have affection physically or verbally. Teresa's mother worked and helped pay the bills and cooked and cleaned for the family.

Teresa said her mother didn't have the mother/daughter talk about "the birds and the bees." She had an older sister and they were close.

Teresa said that she had a baby and her parents were not pleased at all, but they loved the baby. Her mother was supportive when Teresa fell in love with another young man and tried to make the relationship work but it was to no avail. He was very abusive. She had moved to another town and had to return home with more children. Teresa remembered how much her mother loved the children and how supportive they were with the children.

Teresa described her mother as being strong and is grateful that she also has that trait! She also said that her mother taught her children how to be strong as well.

Teresa took care of her parents and said that she was doing all that she could for them, as they had done for them.

Teresa has two daughters and two sons. She is affectionate and tells them they are loved. The advice she gave them is that life is not easy, that it is a test and to pray and believe in themselves.

Tilia

Tilia was one of seven siblings, three boys and four girls, with the last of the girls being a set of twins!

According to Tilia, she was not close to her mother, and there was no warmth or affection, and displayed anger issues.

Tilia quit high school and de-scribed going down the wrong path and eventually ending up in prison. She made the decision to change her life and finished school, married, and had two sons and one daughter. Tilia remained estranged from her mother and later realized her mother was suffering from bipolar depression. She said the man she married began exhibiting angry behavior and was also diagnosed with bipolar depression.

Tilia said that her husband agreed to get help and received anger management therapy and is doing so much better.

Both Tilia and her husband are affectionate towards their children. She said that when her five-year-old daughter becomes angry, besides talking with her and time outs, Tilia's husband gives her an old phone book or magazine and she's allowed to tear it up, with one stipulation - that she picks up the pieces!

Brittney

Brittney said she was the firstborn of three children. She described growing up as fun, and active, and how there was "never a dull moment!" Her mother supported all types of extracurricular activities.

Brittney explained how her mother was strict, but made sure she and her siblings knew right from wrong.

"We were disciplined when needed." They were explained to why they were being disciplined. Brittney stated they got along well then and now. She described holidays as fun and all about family and socializing. Brittney is grateful to her mother for having taught her fun things like "how to sew, crochet, hand stitch, cook, be responsible, and how to survive with very little!"

She loved the way they had openness and closeness with her mother. Brittney did not like it when her mother was disappointed or angry with her.

Brittney has four daughters and is teaching them responsibility, hygiene, cooking, cleaning, and how to be respectful to others.

Lori

Lori is the third of five children. According to Lori, she had a wonderful childhood but was not allowed to play outside!

"My parents were very overprotective."

Lori described the family as being poor but happy as they may not have had a beautiful home, but they never went without.

Lori's mother was a stay-at-home mom and made sure Lori and her siblings had three healthy meals a day.

Lori explained that her mom could be mean if they made her mad, such as coming home late!

Lori stated she got along with her mom well unless she didn't do what her mom told her to do or not to do! "She would pull my hair because she didn't like certain guys I dated, especially after she had expressed how she didn't like them!"

Lori remembered how her mom would make noise and bang dishes and things to wake her up early if she had come home late. Her dad didn't appreciate her making noises and would become loud and verbal with her mom!

Lori has one daughter that she is very proud of. Her daughter has a college degree and Lori has taught her to be independent and to never depend on a man to complete her.

Avita #1

"I have three children, two girls, and a boy. We traveled to Mexico to see Mom a few times.

Mama illegally came back to the States and I invited her to stay with my children and me.

Mama became offended that I had invited her to stay with me. She stated that she could not picture herself living in a trailer, as I was then, renting a nice single-wide trailer. Mama also said that she had too many pretty things and the chandelier, and where would she place all these things if she lived with me? My children didn't see Mama as a grandmother and Mama didn't have the grand-mother bond.

"It seemed like my older sister had also become very materialistic and she and I grew apart as a result, while she and Mama grew closer.

"There was a time when I was down on my luck, as my car was on its last leg and trying to raise three children as a single mom. My mama, of course, could not help me, and my sister flat-out refused to assist in any way. My sister sabotaged my chance at purchasing a vehicle. She was also calling Mama and giving her misinformation and usually, Mama didn't have the grand-mother bond.

"It seemed like my older sister had also become very materialistic and she and I grew apart as a result, while she and Mama grew closer.

"There was a time when I was down on my luck, as my car was on its last leg and trying to raise three children as a single mom. My mama, of course, could not help me, and my sister flat-out refused to assist in any way. My sister sabotaged my chance at purchasing a vehicle. She was also calling Mama and giving her misinformation and usually their conversations were negative and about me.

"I went to x-ray school and began to make life better for my children and myself.

"My children were growing up and my teenage daughter began to rebel because, apparently, I was too strict! By that time, I realized that I wanted to be different from my mama. I wanted to pay attention to my children and didn't want them to grow up as I had. Of course, my daughter disagreed, and she became defiant and begged to go live with her father in another town.

"I worried day and night and would go see her when I could.

My ex-husband was never around and my daughter was left alone, or with friends, most of them men.

"My teenage daughter was into drugs and sex and after one year, returned home. She had been through really tough times and realized that she needed her mama after all.

"Now my second born is a teenager and is accusing me of being too strict, and does not want to follow the rules. Despite talks, being grounded, and having her phone taken away, nothing has worked, I will keep trying, though, and not give up!

"I have also forgiven my mother. I do love her very much and understand some of her behavior now. Mama wanted to be free and find true love. She is free and has embraced being alone. Mama is still in Mexico, has a good job, and makes a fairly decent living. The other day, she called me and said she didn't have any heat for a while. Then she added, 'Lucky for me I'm wearing my fur coat and staying warm!' Oh, and she still has her beautiful chandelier!"

Avita #2

"I was the third born of four children. We were two girls and two boys. My father brought my mother from Mexico. My dad sold drugs and eventually went to prison. Mama took over dad's business selling drugs and very quickly got caught and went to jail. We were cared for by relatives.

"My oldest brother also got into the drug business and went to prison. Mama became a different person. She had been the submissive wife, raising four children and not having any friends, far away from her family, and not having much of a life outside of the house.

"Mama began going out with friends she had made and soon remarried. The man that she married bought her the material things she had only dreamed of having. This man also liked other women and they argued all of the time and he was physical with her!

"Mama divorced him.

"By that time, my older sister married young and I was a teenager with no mother at home, attention, rules, or love, so I used drugs, became sexually active, and I became an angry teenager. I recall the abusive names I used to scream out at Mama and how my brothers had to restrain me from physically attacking my mama!

"Mama resumed her bad relationships and made out like a bandit, with jewelry, name-brand furniture, and clothes! Mama made sure she took all her pretty things with her after she would leave each man.

Mama would even pack and un-pack her beautiful chandelier and take it with her! Mama continued selling drugs, though, and was eventually deported back to Mexico."

Korine

"My mother and I were never close. I was the baby of eight siblings, four girls and four boys. I guess my mother was too tired from raising so many children! Some of my older brothers and sisters began to leave home for college and work. When they would come home to visit, they would make comments about how 'weird' I acted.

"The truth is that my mother and I had never bonded, and I certainly never felt love or affection. I had food, shelter, clothes, and pets to occupy myself with. I had some female acquaintances, and one best friend, who also thought that I was odd.

"When I was five years old, my biological father began to sexually abuse me. I never told my mother or my siblings. My father told me not to tell, so I erased it from my memory as much as I could. Growing up, I was withdrawn, hard to get along with, and untrusting.

"I was not close to either of my parents or to anyone else for that matter. My father continued to allow me to buy the most expensive clothes and shoes that I wanted. It still wasn't enough! I still felt 'ugly and unworthy.'

"I dated guys and eventually married and moved out of state. My marriage wasn't working out and I began counseling. It was actually through my counseling that the sexual abuse resurfaced. My counselor had me write a letter to my father (as part of my therapy) to let him know how he had ruined my life. I wrote the letter, and let him know how he had taken away my innocence, childhood, happiness, and probably any chance of any kind of happiness with any man. My father received the letter and my mother, who also read it, said he cried, but I never received an 'I'm sorry' from them.

"In actuality, my mother resented me more and my father never mentioned anything. My mother did mention it to some of my siblings and of course, they didn't believe it. Four of my sisters are professionals in the health field and only one believes me.

"I am divorced now, and try to maintain a good relationship with my adult child and my siblings. Both of my parents are now deceased and I have forgiven them, but I am not able to forget. Please don't turn the other cheek if you know this is happening to your child, relative or otherwise. It is your obligation to intervene, report and stop the abuse!"

Korine goes to therapy and is now divorced. Every day is a struggle for her and she has good and bad days. She loves to encourage others. Korine tries to stay close to her daughter who is not open to any kind of relationship.

Priscilla

"I was the middle child. My brother was the eldest, then my sister, and I was the baby. We were brought up very strict, but we knew we were loved! Notice I'm saying, 'knew.' I personally do not recall a hug or an 'I love you' from my parents. Aunts and uncles hugged me and commented nice things or at times, not-so-nice comments!

"My mother was one of ten children. My maternal grandmother was mean and never showed me or my sister any attention or affection. She would 'shoo' the girls away from her house, but would let the grandsons, especially my brother, stay and she would even take him on trips with her.

"I suppose that mother, in a way, was very much like her. Mother was much younger than Daddy and they had the three of us one year after the other. Daddy worked and mother stayed home. They both cooked and mother loved decorating and having the house nice and tidy.

"Growing up was not bad, but my mother disliked most of my boyfriends, especially if they were Hispanics! (We are Hispanics.) My mother was half German because my grandmother was German. Mother wanted three of us to marry Anglo men and for my brother to many an Anglo woman. I liked Hispanic guys but when my mother found out, I was forbidden to have anything to do with them!

"I did meet an Anglo man, married him, and went to live out of state. Mom visited twice and came to stay with me when I had my baby. Ten years went by, and my husband turned out to be a womanizer and a drunk. We divorced and I remarried again and again. It was like 'deja vu!'

"My sister also married an Anglo man and he also was a terrible husband and father!

"But I'm not saying that Anglo men are bad, ok? My sister and I were unlucky, that's all. My brother married a Hispanic girl and they are still married,

"I wish that I had lived close to Mom and that I had been able to tell her about my feelings and my life, but back then, when you were married and had left home, you were told, 'You stay married, and if you have problems, you work them out.' So, I tried.

"Being a single mom, I tried to teach my daughter to be strong and not depend on anyone. Thank God she is strong and stands up for what she believes!"

Draya

Draya was the baby of four children. She has two brothers and one sister; two of her brothers are now deceased. Her older brother and sister had already left home and were living out on their own. Draya and her other older brother were still in school.

Draya's mother was mostly a stay-at-home mom. She did work for a while. Draya recalls her mom being particular about cleanliness and the home was spotless and everything was placed where it belonged. Her mom was very meticulous about her appearance and Draya's as well.

Draya remembers her mom stressing the importance of personal hygiene, clean clothing, combed hair, etc. Draya's dad was a musician and played in a band. He did not have any other employment.

Draya said that she had a normal childhood. Her mom cooked and cleaned and took care of the family. Draya remembered how there were times when there was not enough money, and Draya was not able to go to the movies or buy toys. Other times there was money to do the things that she wanted to do.

Draya got along well with her mom and accepted her lifestyle and was raised in the barrio. When Draya was in high school, she got pregnant and her father died. Draya's boyfriend began dating another girl and denied that he was the father.

Draya recalls how her mother and father argued about her going out and feared she would get pregnant. Draya's mother did talk to her about being careful.

Her oldest brother also died and Draya's mom began to show signs of depression.

She had been exhibiting depressive behavior since her father passed away.

The brother that had remained at home had died in a fire and Draya said her mom became unbearable to live with and was diagnosed with bipolar depression and schizophrenia. Draya said that her behavior was bizarre and that there was no talking her out of anything once she be-came fixated on her beliefs.

Draya said that she would become frustrated with her mom but realized that she was ill and couldn't help it. They would make up until the next episode.

Draya's mom was a good grandmother to Draya's daughter and the daughter was aware of her grandmother's illness.

Draya has a good relationship with her daughter and taught her to be independent. Her mother passed away two years ago and Draya misses her terribly, but she tries to focus on the good times.

Ruthie

Ruthie's mom married at the young age of fourteen, and Ruthie was born two years later. Her parents divorced a year later.

When Ruthie was two years of age, her mother was hanging around people that her parents did not approve of. On one occasion, Ruthie's mom was at a motorcycle rally and two-year-old Ruthie was wandering around unattended and was almost hit by a motorcycle. Her mother didn't react much, but somehow her grandparents became aware of the near-fatal incident and made sure that Ruthie spent a lot more time with them.

When Ruthie was three years old, her mother remarried. Her stepdad actually treated Ruthie okay. Ruthie lived with her mom and stepfather in another state and Ruthie spent holidays and summer vacations with her grandparents, She loved her grandparents and they loved her. They partly raised her.

Ruthie was eight years old when they moved back to her birth state, and her siblings, two sisters and one brother, were born, Ruthie was close to her siblings, but she couldn't help but notice how different she was being treated by her mother. As she got older, the sibling relationship faded and they grew apart.

Growing up, Ruthie longed for a normal teenage daughter/mother relationship, but sadly, it was not to be. Ruthie was blamed for her mother marrying young, not finishing high school and anything else that had gone wrong in her mother's life.

"I needed my mom to care, and she did not!" If she asked her mom if she could go out with her friends or go out on a date, Ruthie's mom would reply, "I don't give a damn what you do, go ask your daddy! If it wasn't for you, I wouldn't have this terrible life!"

Ruthie stated that her mom was very talented and had taught herself to sew and taught me how to sew as well!

"Mom did make me some cool-looking outfits!"

Ruthie said that her mom never realized how independent and self-reliant she taught her to be.

Ruthie had a few relation-ships, and some were not good.

She is presently married and works hard at making it work!

Ruthie informed me that she kept up with her mom through her siblings, and had not seen her mom for twenty years. Recently, though, Ruthie's mom became gravely ill and Ruthie went to see her out of state. Ruthie's mother appeared to be happy to see her. Her mother passed away a few days after the visit.

"I have no children, so I guess that it was not in the cards for me, but I also know that I would have been much different if I had!"

Ann

"I was the oldest of three sisters. I am three years older than the middle sister, and eight years older than the youngest sister. I don't remember any-thing before age seven, but 1 do have many pictures in my mind from ages 7 to 11 of certain family members, friends, scenarios, and events. I remember the elementary school that I at-tended and the railroad tracks that I used to walk on when going home from school.

"I lived in the country and we walked a lot as we didn't own a car. We lived within walking distance of two other houses, one where my paternal grandparents lived and also my uncle, his wife, and their four children. One of the kids was about my age and the others were younger. In the other house lived my father's uncle, his wife, and their son who was eight years older than me. We were all very close. The houses were walking distance apart, perhaps maybe a thousand feet apart.

"The scenery was beautiful. I remember the palm trees, the mango and banana trees, and the stream that was near our home that would always flood after the torrential tropical rainstorms. I remember playing and bathing there with my sisters and my cousins. It was such fun! I distinctly remember the wonderful sound and smell of the rain, and it is still a very pleasant memory.

"There was an unpaved road that was only four-hundred feet from our home that led to the main paved road. There, we would catch a bus into town where our other family lived, as well as where a few stores were located.

"I remember we had no electricity and none of the modern luxuries that we see today.

"The fragrance of the rose flower garden my mother had was out of this world, especially after a nice evening breeze. Nighttime was beautiful. I felt I could touch the stars with my hands, and the moon was big and bright; it was our faithful companion.

"As children, we would run and play outside, play games like hopscotch, jump rope, etc. We would chase and capture fireflies and place them in jar containers.

"While we were indoors, we would play board games, and jacks, and when adults and children gathered, we would sing and recite poetry.

"The adults sat on rocking chairs and spacious covered front porches. They would laugh and applaud our plays and presentations. Everything we ate was freshly cooked that same day, as we didn't own a refrigerator. One of my jobs as a child was chasing the chickens to see where they would lay their eggs!

"My mother would get up very early in the day to wash our clothes by hand. She would sing out loud as she washed and hung the clothes with clothespins, clean, cook, sew, embroider, and iron.

"We had limited possessions, but everything we had was clean, treasured, and cared for as a valuable possession. Our few clothes and shoes were designated as our casual and dressy attire, and we dared not to mix the two! Our dresses were handmade and embroidered by my mother.

"I remember eating a lot of different tropical fruit right off the fruit trees. Oranges, grapefruit, mangoes, guavas, and coconuts were just a few of these wonderful fruits.

"Pets were always kept out-side the house, never indoors.

"We celebrated birthdays and holidays with roasted pigs and the typical ethnic food of white rice, black beans, fried bananas, etc. We would drink fresh milk from the cows that were milked early in the morning. The butter was also homemade and delicious!

"My grandfather owned the acres of land surrounding us as well as fields of sugar cane. We loved eating the freshly cut sugar cane. So, so sweet! I also remember chasing butterflies after watching them grow through their different stages.

"I remember memorizing the multiplication tables. I would follow my mother around the house as she did her chores. She would say '1x1' and I would reply, '1' and so on. At an early age, my mom had me memorize poems. At age four; I had memorized all the stages of 'Los Zapaticos de Rosa,' by Jose Marti. (A very long poem by a famous poet.)

"My mom has always been a hard worker. She was very dedicated to her jobs as a homemaker, wife, and mother. She has always believed in cleanliness.

"My mom was creative, honest, giving, and physically active. She has always had a lot of energy! Mom took pride in her work, her husband, and her family.

"I always admired and respected my mother. My appreciation for her has grown immensely throughout the years. I consider her my best friend, the only person in the world (besides God) who loves me unconditionally, who rejoices in my accomplishments, and who encourages me and gives me strength when I am sad.

"My mom is my rock and the best role model in my life. I love my mom's inner strength and courageous spirit, and her faith in God. She is genuinely a good human being, always thinking of giving and serving others.

"My mom never leaves a task to be done in the future if it can be done today. She is very disciplined. My mom is also blunt and talks a lot! She can also be passive-aggressive and controlling. She wants and demands things to be done well and 'right away!'

"My mom has taught me that a sense of duty to self, family, and others is very important, Cleanliness is next to Godliness, how other people see us is important, so we need to watch what we say and do. Respect and kindness are also important. Respect and kindness are of the utmost importance.

"My mom has also taught me to never, never give up doing what is right. Also, everyone goes through ups and downs in life, but we can't stay down, we must get up and keep going! Most importantly, that faith in God is essential!

Mom also taught me that giving and caring is our duty and it should come from the heart, to stay active and busy at all times, be honest, follow the Ten Commandments, not mingle with the wrong crowd, and stay away from bad people and bad situations.

"She also taught us other things as well, such as you need to place things back in their place, a neat and organized house looks clean and is easier to keep up, never stop learning or trying, and for goodness' sake, clean those baseboards!

"I have two daughters. I had my first one at age 23 and the second at age 29. I am not sure what I have taught them. They are both so different. One day I will ask them!

"However, I would like to think that I taught them to be strong, and to see, know and follow God.

"Also, to be honest, to have integrity, to get an education, to be humble and respectful, and to get a good job so they don't have to depend on any man.

"Other things are to be clean, organized, and creative, to remember family is very important, and to be proud of their culture, who they are, their language, and their beliefs, Also, to know that they are not better than anyone else, but no one else is better than they are, I hope and pray that I have taught them to be kind, thoughtful, and respectful, to stay away from trouble and obey the law, to travel the world, and to gain a greater understanding of others, their culture, their language, their foods, and their beliefs.

"Also, don't lie, steal, and don't envy anyone. Believe in God and pray about everything. Love and respect others as you respect yourself, read the Bible, and follow God's teachings; there is another life for the soul beyond this present life. Go to church! Remember to love and forgive yourself and others and always remember everyone makes mistakes. Those who bring you down are not your friends. Never give up, and if you fall, get up and keep going!

You can't change the past but you can change the future by what you choose to do and control today."

Magdalena

Magdalena is the third of four siblings, and she is the only female. Magdalena grew up in the Jehovah's Witness religion and they did not celebrate holidays. They did have family time and would play sports, build model planes, and fly them. Tennis, bowling, and volleyball as well as softball were also enjoyed as a family.

Her mom was a stay-at-mom and taught them how to grow gardens, sew, cook, and clean.

They also would chop cotton and later owned and managed a janitorial business and lastly a vitamin/health products business as well as a massage business.

Magdalena considers her mom a smart woman even though she had no formal schooling. "I can only imagine what all she would have accomplished if she had!"

Magdalena said her mother continues to be motherly with them, plus has taken in others that didn't get motherly attention.

Magdalena has two daughters and said she gets along well with them. She described the daughters as "millennials" and herself as a "baby boomer." Magdalena stated they can talk about anything with each other. She has taught them all she could about life and they continue to support each other.

Magdalena said her mother has taught her to be compassionate and generous, and has been exemplary and a real-life lesson for her. She stated she intends to pass this on to her daughters.

Missy

Missy said she is the eighth of twelve siblings. "I have four older brothers, four younger brothers, and three older sisters, so I am the baby girl!" Growing up was both good and bad according to Missy. She referred to the bad being due to there not being enough money for the large family.

The good part of growing up was that she and her siblings were loved and her parents did the best they could. Missy stated she got along well with her mother, but when she became a teenager, they bumped heads! Missy explained, "I thought I knew everything!"

She described how the holidays were "always wonderful!"

Missy loved her mom's meals, and said, "She was the best cook and she would cook the most delicious meals out of nothing!" Missy learned how to cook like her mother.

Missy remembered how her mother would read books to her and her siblings. Her mother was involved in PTA and involved in the children's (she and her siblings') school activities. "My mother wasn't the best housekeeper but with twelve kids, I totally under-stand!"

She stated there is nothing about her mother that she would change. "She did so much for us and did without so that we could have what we needed." Missy has three sons, no daughters, but she does have one granddaughter, and she has taught her how to cook and be respectful, polite, and to be respectful and treat others the way she wants to be treated.

Missy said that her sons were also taught these values.

Never wish them pain.

That's not who you are. If they caused you pain, they must have pain inside. Wish them healing.

- Najura Zebian

"Even in her final days, my mom and I had a 'sister support' with each other. We shared secrets, she was the best listener and the best shoulder to lean on. We could shop all day together and never tire of what we were doing! Mom loved my Tejano music and dancing with me. She was my everything and is immensely missed."

Violetta

Violetta was the third born of four children. "There were two girls and two boys. My older brother and sister were married young and lived out on their own.

"My mother was not really close to any of us. She was submissive to my abusive father. I suspect that my older siblings witnessed my father abusing my mother and couldn't wait to leave home.

"My father was both verbally and physically abusive to me. My mother was not allowed to stop it or to intercede in any way. Once, my father even broke a broom across my back.

I could not understand how a mother would not defend her children. Therefore, my mother never formed a mother/daughter bond with me and I never felt the connection that I wanted to have been able to feel.

"I remember begging my mother to leave my father and move us back to Puerto Rico, but she said that she couldn't because she was afraid of my father. My mother then admitted that my father would beat her also.

"I felt hopeless and at the age of fourteen, I met a twenty-one-year-old man and I moved in with him. This man and I were more like roommates, but I got pregnant and I gave birth to a baby girl.

"The man didn't work and did not do much of anything. I worked cleaning houses and I paid the rent and the bills, and I bought baby needs!

"My mother knew where I was and told my father, and he asked me to return home.

"I refused because I knew that he would beat me and now I had a baby. I had little communication with my mother and I finally asked the man to leave after several years".

Violetta said that she continued to work and she raised her daughter by herself.

Violetta discovered that she liked to work in sales and is still working to this day.

Her daughter is now twenty years old and Violetta expressed how close they are and how she and her daughter can talk about anything. Violetta said that she has raised her daughter to be kind, honest, and strong. Violetta stated that her daughter is in a good relationship with a nice guy and does not hesitate to ask for advice if needed. She also states that she is her daughter's mother and best friend.

Violetta said that she has forgiven her father for her own good, but she also has no contact with him. Violetta said that her mother eventually did return to Puerto Rico and that she stays in contact with her but has no loving feelings to-wards her at all.

Megan

Megan is the third born of six siblings. She is the middle child and stated, "The middle child syndrome is pretty much as is defined!" Megan described her-self as growing up, doing what she was told to do, plus what the other siblings weren't told to do. The older siblings didn't have chores to do because they were older, and the younger ones weren't asked to do them because they were babies, "So that left me!" Megan said.

Megan described her relationship with her mother as being, at times, "full of resentment." She believed that her mother perceived Megan as her rival. Megan stated that she had no idea why her mother was so different with her.

Megan loved her mother and was respectful and knew she had to do better and be better, in order to be recognized by her mother. There was no mother/daughter relationship. She longed for closeness with her mother, but instead, she would hear her mother telling others, "She is the black sheep." Megan remembered how hurt she was!

Megan was not allowed to hang around with friends and was not allowed to date like other teenage girls and that didn't help the relationship with her mother any!

She said that as she grew older, she did realize that she "tipped the edge!" Megan explained how she had eloped in her senior year of high school, while her other siblings all had church weddings.

Megan said that she was grateful to her mother for holding on to the reins, otherwise, she wouldn't be who she is today!

Megan said that meal traditions were based on Christian holidays, Tamales for Christ-mas, Easter egg hunts, and turkey with all the trimmings on Thanksgiving. Megan kept these traditions that she loves so much!

Megan's mother had little education, yet she taught herself to read, sew and drive. Her mother was a confident lady and also joined a group of all-white senior dancers. She was the only Hispanic! Megan explained that although she herself does not have the kind of confidence that her mother had, she strove to be better for herself, and she obtained a degree where she ended up working in a leadership role.

Megan says that she loves life and has instilled the traditions, values, and importance of her love for Christ in her daughter. According to Megan, she at tributes her Christian faith to her mother.

Joanna

"I am the middle child of two older and two younger siblings, and I am also the only female. Growing up, we were poor but had what we needed.

"Mom and I were closer when I was little, but not so much after I got older. I was definitely closer to my dad.

"My mom was very strict! I did like that my mom was a hard worker and taught me to be the same. She taught me how to cook and make tortillas when I was nine years old. I am a lot like my mom, very hard-headed!

"I have no daughter but I taught my sons how to cook, clean, wash clothes, and every-thing they needed to be good men! I am very proud of them!"

Joanna is grateful for everything her mother taught her and they did have an okay relationship.

Tiara

Tiara was the firstborn of three siblings. Her mother was seventeen years old when Tiara was born. Tiara's aunt picked up Baby Tiara from the hospital due to her mother wanting to leave her at the hospital. Her aunt took Baby Tiara to her grandparents, who ended up raising her. Tiara would visit her mother on occasion, but there was no sign of affection and she was scared to death of her mother. Tiara explained that her mother slept with "a big knife under her pillow!"

Tiara's grandparents were of a religion that didn't celebrate holidays, birthdays, or anything else, so Tiara didn't know why her family didn't have fun times as other families did.

"As I was growing up, I realized that I had a party mom."

Tiara witnessed her mother selling and doing drugs. Eventually, her mother was arrested and sentenced to prison for a year and a half. During her mother's prison time, she gave birth to a baby boy.

Tiara never became close to her mother. She has tried to teach her daughter to be strong, loving, and resilient.

Charlie

Charlie is the baby of five siblings. According to Charlie, growing up was difficult. She said that her mother married young and was in an abusive marriage (both verbally and physically).

Charlie said that her three oldest siblings grew up with their maternal grandparents and that they harbored resentment towards Charlie, their brother, and their mother.

According to Charlie, they still do to this day. Charlie said that she gives her mother credit for trying to love them all the same but she and her brother felt and could tell who was "loved more and who were the least favorite." Charlie remembered that her mother had a hard time hiding it.

She describes herself as rebellious and running away to try to get away from her family lifestyle and everything that was happening.

Charlie became pregnant and married an African American man and that placed more distance between them since "my mother cared about what other people thought and what family would say."

Charlie said holidays were happy when her stepdad was around, but after her mother and he divorced, it became bad because her mother, her sib-lings, and her grandparents did not get along. Someone would say or do something, and it would never end well.

Charlie said that she liked her mom's bluntness, strength, and ambition. "She can be the sweetest person or your worst enemy!" Charlie stated. Charlie said her mother was stubborn and would not admit to being wrong, even when she was.

Charlie explained how she is grateful for her mother teaching her independence as she left on her own and made it on her own.

Charlie is the opposite of her mother in that she is caring, loving, and affectionate. She said that she listens to her kids and she loves them on a daily basis. Her mother adores Charlie's kids!

Charlie has two daughters and they get along well and are loving and kind. Like any other siblings, they disagree from time to time, but they ultimately resolve whatever is going on between them. She has taught them to be respectful, respect themselves, and to "Be happy! Life is short. You are young today and old tomorrow. Learn to listen and talk without screaming! Everyone has special God-given gifts and talents. Seek and find yours!"

Gracie

Gracie is the third child of five siblings. She said that she had a rough upbringing because her mother had to work to help make ends meet, as her father, she said, "made bad doings."

Gracie remembers having little clothes and food. She explains how her mother did the best that she could for all five of her children.

Gracie had to quit school, though, in order to take care of the younger siblings because her mother had to work. She admires her mother for being a hard worker and doing the best that she could. Gracie regrets watching her mother put up with her father, but he did contribute to buying groceries. Gracie said that holidays were so miserable, especially Christ-mas time, with no gifts ever.

Gracie admitted that she didn't have a close mother/daughter relationship, but she did love her mother. On the other hand, Gracie despised her father. Her mother was sub-missive and the man was the boss of the home. Gracie said that she couldn't get past his lies and bad behavior.

Gracie has one daughter and she has taught her to take care of herself, her family, and to also help others. She has also taught her daughter to be kind and to love deeply.

Rosey

"I was the third girl born of twelve children. There were six boys and six girls.

"Growing up was quite different from our school-mates.

"My father kept us in a secluded environment in order to be free of drugs, alcohol, and falling victim to the world. We thought that it was great because we didn't know any better.

"I had a wonderful relation-ship with my mother. Mother was a stay-at-home mom who cared for all of us kids. Her re-sources were limited, but again, she did the best that she could.

"I always wondered how Mom and Dad made it through the holidays. We would all get two gifts that weren't really much, but they meant the world to me! I was always so grateful.

"What I liked best about Mom was the way she set her foot down so I could attend college and stay away from be-coming a migrant worker. Mom had our backs without a doubt. One of the things I did not like was not being able to date. Therefore, I married without really knowing other options that I could have had out in the world.

As of today, there is not one thing that I would change about my mother. I loved her for all she did for me! Mom taught me wisdom beyond reproach. Despite her limits on her education, she was a genius!"

Sara

Sara was the second born, and she had a brother a year older than her. Sara was born in Massachusetts. Her parents had a bad marriage, and Sara's bio-logical father was an alcoholic. Her mother told her husband she was going to visit her sick father out of state, and she did go see her ailing father and also got divorced via mail!

Sara's mother didn't return to Massachusetts. Sara was two years old. Her mother went to work at the phone company and one day she went out on a blind date with a man she immediately did not like because he was a "practical joker!"

The joker obviously became bearable and her mother married him! He was to become the stepfather that she called her one and only father. Apparently, her stepdad's first wife was killed in a tragic car accident and Sara's step-sister-to-be was also in the car and was only a small child. Her parents had a baby and Sara said that she became the middle child.

Sara said as she was growing up, her sister was dating a Hispanic male. Her sister was going to marry a Hispanic guy and her father was very prejudiced. Sara's mother did not have any say so. Her mother was "passive and submissive."

Sara was fifteen years old and demanded that everyone attend the wedding. Everybody went to wish her sister good luck.

Her sister and husband smoked pot, drank, and did acid and other drugs. Sara and her older brother began abusing drugs as well.

When Sara was in her senior year, she was kicked out of the house and she lived out on her own, sometimes with other people, and worked as a dancer or anything else to keep herself fed and clothed.

Sara continued to abuse drugs. She contracted hepatitis and became very ill. Her mother allowed her to return home and nursed her back to health,

Sara went to rehab a few times and decided she was going to make a difference in her life. She went to nursing school and became an RN.

Sara married and gave birth to a son. Her marriage didn't work out and several years later, she remarried a Hispanic man. Her parents attended the wedding. Her father passed away and her mother was not the same. She was so accustomed to her husband making all of the decisions and being taken care of. Sara grew even closer to her mother and talked to her and visits her daily.

Sara's mother depends on her even though she has two other daughters. The oldest of Sara's sisters died after complications of prolonged drug use.

Sara continues to be a care-giver to her mother and is a great role model to her female family members.

Terry

"My mother Kitty died when I was five years old. She had a bad heart. I was second to the youngest out of eight siblings. My sisters raised me, and we were very close. Ever since my mother died, I have always felt her presence with me, guiding me, bringing me messages in dreams, in which she would appear and we would have con-versations, or else she would foretell future family events!"

Terry explained that she has always had premonitions and she had been told by her family that her mother was also very perceptive like her.

"Another time in a dream, mother and I were looking in-side a closet, and observed two sets of dresses, shoes, sweaters, and pants, and then Mother asked me 'Poo, do you know what this means? It means your cousin is having twins!' My cousin did actually give birth to twin girls!"

Terry's family told her stories about her mother and about her lifestyle and it was similar to hers!

On one occasion, Terry's friend was coming for a visit and they had worked out all of the details. Her friend didn't show up at the estimated time so, naturally, Terry became worried. She had a feeling that something was really wrong. She got in her car, drove on the road where her friend was sup-posed to be traveling on, got out of her car, and felt the sudden urge to walk toward the cliff!

Terry stated, "I looked down the cliff and saw a body! It wasn't a steep hill so I began to climb down and I found my friend lying at the bottom of the cliff with her dog by her side. She had fallen off the cliff while she was chasing her dog!" After my friend had recovered, she told me, "Kitty was here with me!" Kitty was Terry's mother.

Out of all seven siblings, two of her brothers and two of her sisters died from pulmonary fibrosis. One of her brothers died from pulmonary fibrosis after receiving chemotherapy, and the second brother died later from pulmonary fibrosis also. He had been a Navy Seal. Terry's sister also died from the same illness. Her younger sister also was diagnosed with pulmonary fibrosis, and later Terry was also.

Terry's sister is in remission, but Terry was on oxygen and was hopeful for a lung trans-plant. Her family was asked to participate in a genetic study and it was confirmed that it was genetic and lay dormant and certain factors and conditions allowed the illness to manifest. Terry's strength, she claims, comes from her mother! Terry is close to her daughter and has taught her to be strong and never give up.

Makayla

"I am the youngest of two sib-lings," said Makayla. "I would describe my relationship with my mother as a "roller coaster ride!"

Holidays were great when Makayla was a child. Her great-grandmother and grandmother cooked delicious meals that included tamales for Christmas, and turkey and dressing for Thanksgiving and Easter.

Christmas was Makayla's favorite time as the family would all congregate at her great grandmother's and her grandmas later on. Makayla's grandmother took over and planned all the holidays after her great-grandmother passed away.

She liked the fact that her mother defended her and protected her whether Makayla was right or wrong, but "I don't like the person she's turned into today!" Makayla explained that her mother's lifestyle is questionable and inappropriate. According to Makayla, she learned not to ever be like her mother. Makayla stated she hopes to be a good and loving grandmother someday!

She said she has a beautiful five-year-old daughter who is just like her! Makayla added that she will teach her daughter and son to love, to be brave, and to believe that anything they set their minds to do, can be done! Makayla makes sure her children know that "Mama will always be there!"

Yo

Yo said when her parents married, her father had custody of his five-year-old daughter from a previous marriage. Shortly after, Yo was born, and then her two brothers. Yo stated she was ten years old when her parents adopted another little girl.

According to Yo, her mother was a very strong, domineering, and possessive woman of Yo and her two siblings! Over-all, though, Yo said she and her mother got along well, that is, until she started dating! Her mom didn't want Yo and her siblings to date just one specific person because she was afraid that they would fall in love and marry too young. Yo's mother wanted Yo and her siblings to date many people and if they saw the same person more than three times, the mother would make life very "hectic!" Yo described having to sneak out to see the guy if she wanted to date him more than three times! Yo added, "I didn't want to date a lot of guys at the same time. I would be a floosie!" Yo said she ended up eloping with a soldier from the military base and resided out of state.

Her mother was furious and Yo didn't see her parents again for two years. Yo said, "Whew! After that, everything was fine!"

She fondly remembered how the holidays were fun and special. According to Yo, her mother did all the cooking and the girls did all the cleaning.

"Mom never taught us to cook!"

Yo loved that her mom tried to give them everything they asked for but regrets that she didn't give her parents anything in return. After she be-came an adult, Yo did give the parents gifts.

Yo's father passed away first, and later her mother got dementia. Yo asked her to never forget her and the mother said she would not because Yo was her firstborn. Sadly enough, her mother did forget her but recognized other members of the family! Yo concluded with, "I miss both my parents so much."

Christina

Christina is the second of eleven siblings. She remembers being poor but grateful and happy with what they had.

Christina informed me that she was "always a giver, never a taker."

According to her, she was a daddy's girl, which got her in trouble with her sisters.

She also stated that it was not her fault and they just didn't understand. She still felt bad about it though.

Christine fondly recalled how her mother was a stay-at-home mom that was patient and there for them, "no matter what!" She added that her mother was humble, very sweet, and caring. Christina said her mother was calm and quiet and didn't drink alcohol, and Christina stated, "I don't know how she did it because we were more than a handful!" According to Christina, she was one of the oldest and had a lot of responsibilities as her mother didn't drive and only spoke Spanish. Life was simple and happy in her growing-up years, Christina said. Holidays were always happy. Her mom's side of the family celebrated with her parents and siblings, and there was always plenty to eat.

As a family, Christina said they would watch their favorite cartoons, play games, cook, fight, and make up afterward! Her mother was around to guide them. Christina stated they didn't go out of town be-cause the family was so large.

She stated her mother taught her how to keep the house, cook and sew. Christina remembered all the good advice her mother gave her! She loved being close to her mother while they would make "big stacks of tortillas every day!"

Christina has one daughter and granddaughter, and they all get along well. She has taught them to respect and love one another "because family comes first, especially your mom." Christina said both her mom and she have stressed the importance of attending church and keeping the faith.

Amelia

Amelia is the youngest of six siblings. She remembers her growing-up years as "full of laughter." Like most families, Amelia said they had disagreements but worked them out!

Amelia described her mother as a beautiful, strong woman. Her mom was single and worked hard to provide for them. Amelia praised her mother for "never giving up on us!" Amelia said her mom was too strict, but knew she had raised a responsible daughter!

Holidays were fun and laughter with family. Amelia said some sad times in her life were when her brother passed away and when her mother passed at age 84. Amelia has one daughter that she proudly raised with the same values her mother taught her.

Joann

Joann was the first of four siblings (all girls). She was raised by her parents in a home filled with "Lots of Love!" Joann said she got along well with her mom and still does, except her mom calls her Joanna and Joann said, "My name is Joann!"

Joann described her mom as a stay-at-home mom, and her mom taught them how to cook, clean, and iron. According to Joann, she is thankful to her mother for having taught them how to be respectful and to treat others well. Joann also is grateful to her mother for "al-ways being there for us, in case we needed anything."

Holidays were fun, filled with laughter, family, and lots of delicious food prepared and gifts for holidays and birthdays.

Joann has one daughter and she has taught her to be independent, to treat people the way she wants to be treated, to work hard so she will never do without, and to treat her husband and daughters with respect. Joann continues to be close with her mother and siblings.

Lupe

Lupe is the second of eight sib-lings. She said she had an okay childhood, as her mother was very strict. According to Lupe once she got married, they be-came close and they could talk about anything and enjoyed doing things together.

Holidays were fun and the girls assisted the mother with meal preparation, Lupe is thankful to her mother for teaching her how to cook. She enjoys preparing delicious meals for her family and grandchildren!

Lupe's mother was a strong lady and maintained a positive attitude when she became very 111.

Lupe is grateful for taking after her mother! Like her mother, family comes first. Lupe has two daughters and she has taught them to be strong, make their children their priority, stand up for themselves, stay close to their family, and pray.

Ann Marie

Ann Marie is the youngest of five siblings. According to Ann, the family didn't have much money but the parents made sure they were loved.

Ann added, "Our mom was selfless, she always put us before her and went without for us!" Ann said her mother taught them to treat others like they wanted to be treated, rich or poor. Ann remembered how her mother "never took time for herself."

Ann has two daughters and said that they bump heads. She said she told her daughters she was their friend, but a mother first. The daughters didn't understand fully.

Ann taught her daughters how to love one another be-cause after she's gone all they will have is each other. Her daughters are mothers now and Ann gave them the advice to not follow in her footsteps as she informed them that she had made some bad choices in her fife,

According to Ann, these choices affected her daughters. Ann also advised her daughters to be the best moms possible, especially during their early years as they are the most impressionable and important years ever!

Jane

Jane was the youngest of two siblings.

She described her mother as being reserved, but with a very funny, dry sense of humor. She said the whole family has discovered just how funny the mother was since they all quote her often! Jane stated that her mother was a stay-at-home mom, and was quite involved during her growing-up years.

According to Jane, her mother made sure she participated in school activities, church, and the YMCA. "She was the 'boots on the ground' because my daddy was gone much of the time working."

Jane explained how her sister married when she (Jane) was five, so it was pretty much her and her mother. Even though they were very close, her mother encouraged her to be independent. Jane remembers how her mother taught her to pay bills at various stores, and she would go by herself after being taught!

She described how holidays were good, and sometimes were spent at home and quiet, and other times they went to the Fort Worth area where they gathered with extended family on both sides. Jane fondly re-membered traveling to El Paso with her parents and riding around and enjoying many luminaries!

One of Jane's favorite things about her mother was that she was low-key overall. She said she had to behave, but that things were calm most of the time, and that with the expectations, standards were set early on. Jane said she liked the steadiness, reliability, and security of it. Her mother was not a fan of cooking so they ate out a lot, which was fine with Jane!

She also stated that her

mother was like other mothers as far as being strict, not allowing her to go and do everything she wanted to do. Jane realized that most children "go through various stages and ages in varying degrees!" She said she learned a good moral code from her mom that applied to many areas of her life.

Jane has one daughter and they get along well and are very close, and have a great relationship. "I'm her main to-go-to in good times and in bad!" According to Jane, her daughter shares everything with her. She stated they have wonderful discussions about all kinds of topics and Jane treasures it all!

Jane has taught her children to live with "a good moral compass." Even though she had rules and structure, they had a lot of fun and were successful in school and during their adulthood. One of the main things Jane taught her is that they are no better or worse than anyone else, and to be kind and respectful to all.

Carina

Carina was the youngest of five children - three brothers and two sisters. According to Carina, her childhood was very happy and she was close to her mother, father, and siblings.

Carina and her siblings were born and raised in Mexico.

Holidays were happy times filled with joy and family gatherings at her parents' home. Carina described her mother as being a fantastic cook, and said for holidays and special occasions, her mother prepared Mexican meals of asado, tortillas, beans (frijoles and charro), menudo, and other delicious meals and pastries. With Carina being the youngest, she spent more time at home growing up while her siblings were older and living their own lives.

Carina said although she was close to her parents, they did not verbally or physically ex-press affection. She stated that her grandmother lived an un-happy life with her grandfather and her mother had followed in her grandmother's footsteps.

Carina described her mother as being submissive to her husband, often neglecting her own "wants and needs." Carina said that her father was a good man to everyone but her mother.

"My father was a good provider, willing to help anyone in need," and was a loving father to her, but not to her mother.

Carina said that it was just understood that they (she and her siblings) were loved although it was not expressed. She describes how she is like their parents now. Carina laughed and said she must have been her parents' guardian in another life and her parents lovingly agree.

Donna

Donna is the youngest of seven siblings. She described her life as being "chaotic at times, but ideal and wonderful in many ways." Donna said her birth mother became very ill with a brain tumor when Donna was three. Her brain surgery forced her to place Donna and her brother in foster care.

Donna recalled she had three foster moms and "By and large got along with them."

She described her teen years as "being stubborn and emotionally damaged," Donna described each foster home as being different, and that during her early life, her memories were very happy. Donna stated there were lots of people, laughter, cousins, food, and some gifts. What Donna loved best about her biological mother was that she loved Donna unconditionally, and Donna informed she "never doubted that for a moment!"

Her primary foster mom was a WAC, ran a ranch with the assistance of twelve kids, and had been a teacher, and Donna de-scribed her as being very wise, kind, loving, and very strict. Donna expressed how very much she misses her, as well as her birth mother.

She informed me that she had a foster mom in Los Angeles briefly, and Donna stated, "She would remind you of Jessica Rabbitt. She was a voluptuous red-headed woman who was married to a Cuban immigrant. She could sing like a movie star, so there was AL-WAYS music in the house!"

Donna recalled how her first foster mom could be Judgmental, but a lovely woman otherwise. Donna stated that she taught her how to utilize the banks, and how to attain and maintain credit for her benefit.

Mom number one taught her to be frugal, to give to the earth and reap the bounty, livestock management, the reward of giving to others, and the value of education and learning.

She described foster mom number two as being argumentative with her spouse. Donna stated, "I just imagine they had a very passionate love!" She also taught Donna "how amazing the Platters were!" Donna said she was in love with Jimi Hendrix at the time!

Foster mom number three was very cold at times, protecting her feelings, Donna said. She did teach Donna how to sew. She is grateful that her birth mother taught her that love is the best thing you can give your child, and that Jesus loved her.

Donna stated that during her teen years, her last foster mom was easy to talk to and was their church pianist, and "loved the land." Donna regrets that her birth mom was unable to care for her and her brother following her surgery, and said it was not her mom's fault.

Donna concluded with, "God gave me four handsome sons and finally, one precious baby girl. We do get along, but the teen years were hard. She went against everything that I had tried to teach her. Now that she had children, she understands better!" Donna believes in faith, family, country, and the Golden Rule. Donna added, "Maybe I am a better boy mom because beauty and fashion have never been my strong suit!"

Guadalupe Garcia McCall

Guadalupe (Lupita) was born in Mexico. She describes she was born in a little blue home on Avenida Lopez Mateos in Piedras Negras, Coahuila, Mexico. Lupita's mother told her that she was so strong and didn't act like a newborn! She has eight siblings and being the oldest, Lupita took on the role of big sister and assisted her mother in raising her siblings. Lupita and her siblings called their mother, Mami (Mommy). Their mother was close to all of her children and Lupita being the firstborn had a special bond with her mother.

When Lupita was six years old, the family moved to the United States to reside in Eagle Pass, Texas. They all got home-sick for their hometown in Mexico, as they had left their family and friends behind. Lupita's family would travel to Mexico to see their grand-mother and cousins.

Lupita's parents loved planting. Her mother planted roses all the way to the street! Her father Onesimo once planted a mulberry tree so that the family could have shade in their yard. A mesquite tree grew in the middle of her mother Tomasa's rose bushes.

Lupita described her mother pulling the mesquite tree by the roots and getting her fingers pricked, but the tree kept growing back, no matter what! Their father (Papi) told Mami that it was in the tree's nature to be stubborn, as it was a survivor.

Papi found new employment out of town and Lupita began to notice a change in her Mami. She feared there was something else going on with her mother. Lupita was concerned and inquisitive. Ultimately, she found out that her mother had cancer, Mami didn't want the other children to know about her cancer, but a friend of Lupita's spoke about it with others.

Lupita took solace in writing and reading under the strong, resilient mesquite tree that never gave up, just like Lupita!

Meanwhile, Lupita was taking care of Mami, juggling school and drama classes, and generally evolving into her talented and caring self. When Lupita's father took her mother to a hospital for surgery, Lupita was placed in charge of caring for her siblings. Lupita grew up before her time and managed to care for and feed her siblings, even though she would go to bed hungry and worried about where their next meal would come from.

Tomasa (Mami) passed away and left lasting, loving, and caring memories, Lupita's Papi passed away from COVID. Her seven siblings and she remain as close as ever!

Lupita is trained in theater arts and English. She teaches English in a junior high school.

Lupita has written and published poems for adults; written and published books; has been requested for presentations; and is on the panel for the Spirit of Texas (SPOT) reading list.

Priya Patel

Priya was the middle child, and she felt as if she was the most loved of all her siblings. She and her mother were the best of friends, even when as a teenager Priya had many friends. They loved spending time together, cooking, traveling, trying new restaurants, and most importantly shopping! They would go on many shopping trips and mini vacations together.

Priya was able to spend 41 years with her mother before she passed away, and she re-members having a lifetime's worth of love and laughter with her mom. She remembers everything about her mom as if everything happened just yesterday. During the last few years of her mother's life, Priya feels blessed that she and her mother worked together.

Priya learned a lot from her mom, such as learning how to laugh and love with every-thing that she has. She learned how to be a good wife to her husband, a good daughter to her parents, and most importantly, how to be a "superhero mom" like her own mother was to her. Priya has two boys that she tries every day to fill her mother's shoes with. Her boys remind her so much of her mother, and the boys see so much of their grandmother in their mother. They know that their mom had the best example. She feels that is the biggest compliment that she could ever receive in her life.

She is teaching her boys to live a life for others, to respect their elders, and to take care of her parents, just as she did with her parents. Her boys have big hearts, and she does her best to teach them "to love with very ounce of their being and to let hate or anger be like kryptonite."

Priya is a published poet.

Trust only movement. Life happens at the level of events, not of words. Trust movement.

- Alfred Adler

Maya Angelou

My mother's gifts of courage to me were both large and small. The latter are woven so subtly into the fabric of my psyche that I can hardly distinguish where she stops and I begin.

- Maya Angelou

Maya was the second of two siblings. They had been living with the maternal grand-mother who was unaffectionate. Her mother sent Maya and her brother to live with their paternal grandmother. Maya felt anger and resentment to-ward her mother. At age 13 she was raped by a family member and she stopped speaking for a while.

Maya was sent to live with her mother and grew to like her. She described her mother as looking like a beautiful movie star!

Maya called her mother "Lady." Her mother would kiss Maya and tell her she was beautiful. The mother would welcome Maya and her brother every time she wanted to re-turn home.

Before her mother died, Maya spoke to her mother and they were able to hear each other out. Maya told her mother that she had her permission to go if she needed to. Maya's mother told Maya she knew Maya was going to become somebody special in life and in the lives of others. Maya said that day they "Liberated" one another. "We are more alike that unlike" Maya stated "Love Liberates."

Mom and Me and Mom

- Maya Angelou

Family is not always blood. It's the people in your life who want you in theirs, the ones who accept you for who you are, the ones who would do anything to see you smile and who love you no matter what."

- Maya Angelou

Marie Osmond

Marie is the seventh of eight siblings. She is the only girl.

Marie considers her mother as one of the best examples of motherhood. She describes her mother as being a constant light that she could follow, never fearing that she could fall.

Marie's mother was supportive and believed in her and her brothers "She was, is and al-ways will be my guiding light."

Marie's mother, Olive, had a massive stroke in 2002 at the age of 77. She wrote Marie a note that said "I love every breath I take!"

Marie has one daughter and they are close. Her daughter Jessica traveled with her to shows. Just like her mother accompanied Marie to her shows. When Marie and Jessica were looking at pictures, she apologized to her daughter for not being in the pictures. Her daughter said that Marie was there, as she was taking the pictures.

Marie recalled her mother telling her "She's like an hour glass on a table. You think you have it all figured out now. Then, the hour glass gets turned over by something un-expected or a life change. You find yourself having to learn more patience and grow even more as a mother."

Marla stated, "Like sands through the hour glass... these are the days of our parenting lives."

The key is Love, my mother's wisdom, a daughter's gratitude.

- Marie Osmond

Shirley Temple

Shirley was the third of three siblings (two boys). It is stated that she was "groomed" to be a star from infancy. According to Autobiographies Journals written by Shirley, from the age of 31/2 to 5 years old, Shirley talked about a producer sending children that he felt were mis-behaving, including her, to a "black box" to cool off and make money, not play around. As a result, Shirley would get ear infections and eye styes.

Shirley's mother would beg the producer not to make Shirley act when she was ill, but it was to no avail.

Shirley was close to her mother, Gertrude, and stated they had a tight and loving bond.

Shirley had three children -two girls and one boy.

Her daughter Susan de-scribed her mother as being sweet, lovable and very affectionate. Her children all agreed that Shirley was all about motherhood and her husband.

Shirley's last words about her journey in her life were "I've been so blessed."

- Amanda Champagne Meadows, "Closer Magazine"

January 2018

Tina Turner

Anna Mae Bullock was born in Tennessee in 1939 to farmers/sharecroppers Floyd and Zelma Bullock. Anna Mae was the second born of two siblings. She grew up in Nutbush, Tennessee, and experienced her fair share of racism and abandonment but she still just kept on singing! Anna Mae had a love for singing and stardom!!!

According to Anna Mae, her mother and she had an emotionally distant relationship.

Anna Mae said that even as a little girl, her mother showed no love at all towards her. In an interview with Scotland's Daily Record, she informed the reporter that her mother didn't love her, and said, "It was as simple as that!"

Anna Mae was raised by her grandmother after her mother left the family, due to prolonged abuse from her husband. Anna Mae recalled how, every day, she waited for a letter from her mother that just never arrived.

Anna Mae graduated from high school in 1958, and worked as a nurses' aid. After her grandmother died, Anna Mae was reunited with her mother in St. Louis, and soon Anna Mae learned that her mother's feelings toward her had not changed. Her mother died in 1999 and Tina recalls screaming and screaming at receiving the sad news.

Tina's sister Allie was on her own at this time and working in a night club. This is where Anna Mae ended up meeting Ike Turner. He ended up ruling her, physically and emotionally. She would eventually become Tina Turner.

In 1960, Ike and Tina's song, "A Fool in Love," hit #2 on the R&B charts, with the revision of "Proud Mary" originally done by Credence Clearwater Revival.

Tina and Ike had four sons. In 1968, she attempted suicide by swallowing 50 sleeping pills. She had endured so much physical pain and sorrow at the hands of Ike Turner. Eight years later, she finally gathered up the courage to leave, and the rest was history!

I can look back and understand why my karma was the way it was. Good came out of bad. Joy came out of pain!

Tina Turner in her memoir, My Love Story

People Magazine, Commemorative Edition, Tina Turner, the Queen of Rock and Roll (1939-2023)

FOUR GENERATIONS

- Dolores
- Rachel
- Liza
- Kami
- Kyleigh

Dolores

Dolores was the sixth of six siblings, three boys and three girls. They were all born in Mexico. One son was killed in the war. It was hard times during the Depression that affected everywhere, worldwide. Dolores' father worked hard to support the large family. According to the family, her father owned a huge hacienda in town. Do-lores' father was from Spain and her mother was from France. They had attempted to come to the US through Ellis Is-land but were not permitted, so they ended up in Mexico, where they remained until they were able to come to the US.

When Dolores was a young girl, Pancho Villa, the infamous Revolutionary Bandit, would ride into Mexico with his band of soldados. According to Do-lores, she would climb a tall tree just to see Pancho Villa ride in.

She said the church would ring the church bells to alert the pueblo that Pancho and his soldiers had arrived. Dolores said that families already knew who they were to host and entertain for the evening. A meal was served, and sleeping arrangements were made for Pancho and his men. Dolores loved it when Pancho would spend the evening and night at their home. She described how after dinner of a delicious meal her mother would prepare, Pancho and her father would have coffee and chat about the events of the day! Dolores would go into the parlor and sit on Pancho's lap where he would tell her 'Kiddie tales'.

Afterwards, Dolores would say goodnight and the next day after breakfast, Pancho and his men would ride out again. Do-lores loved the holidays and the family celebrated with gifts, food and had a good time!

Dolores loved that her mother was supportive and remained very close.

Rachel

Rachel is the sixth of seven sib-lings. Four brothers and three sisters. She got along well with her mother. Rachel's mother was a stay-at-home mom, and kept the house, cooked, and washed clothes by hand. Her mother taught the girls how to do chores and take care of themselves. The brothers worked chopping cotton from day to the evening.

Rachel's mother was a quiet but funny lady. The father worked hard to maintain the large family. It was understood that Rachel and her siblings were loved. The older male siblings worked and two went into the Army. The oldest one couldn't get into the military because he was flat footed! He did finish high school ad was the first to in his family to graduate!

The mother was very supportive of her children as well as her husband. Rachel's father was a hardworking man and was involved in community activities and was the manager of a baseball team of adults.

He was well-known in the community,

Holidays were fun and though they were a large fam-ily, the father would bring large boxes of apples, oranges, and nuts for the family and the neighborhood at Christmas. The kids would get small gift and ate home cooked holiday meals.

Rachel worked at a dress shop when she was a teenager, as she loved fashion! She helped her mother with purchasing food for the family. The father was killed in a tragic industrial work accident. It was a shock to the family, relatives, and the community.

Rachel's mother remained a widow throughout the rest of her life and passed away at the age of 100. The family doted on the mother for anything and everything!

Liza

Liza is the middle of three sib-lings. She said she had a great childhood. Even though her mother didn't show much love, Liza said it was understood that she and her siblings were loved. The mother was quiet and was a good mother. Holidays were fun and wonderful with gifts, food and family time. The par-ents got divorced and holidays changed.

Her mother remained supportive and they got along well.

"My mother would give you the shirt off of her back." Liza said her mother is a worrier and gets nervous easily. The mother did all the housework and everything for the children, so Liza said they were not taught how to do anything for them-selves. Liza said they didn't agree on everything when she was in her teen years but be-came closer after Liza grew up and had her own children.

She has one daughter and did not have a good relation-ship when her daughter was a teen. Liza described the relationship as 'rocky'. Liza, like her mother, did everything for her daughter. It was then that Liza realized that she was some of the same things as her mother. Discipline, not showing affection. The daughter and Liza's relationship changed for the better after her daughter became a mother. They remain close.

Liza said she has taught her daughter not follow the "Generational course". Liza said her daughter has the chance of breaking cycles and traditions she doesn't like, and make brand new ones of her own!

Kami

Kami is the first born of three siblings. The only female. She described growing up as fun, but hard at the same time. Ac-cording to Kami, she felt that she got in trouble for "dumb little reasons"! Her brothers got away with so much more. Kami stated her mother had higher expectations for her.

Growing up for Kami was nice and fun but annoying be-cause her mother got upset at the littlest of things, and worries too much, making Kami worry all the more. They did not get along very well then.

Kami said holidays were fun and they received gifts and celebrated with other relatives.

Kami stated that her mother may not know, but because of how Kami was treated, she treats her own daughter better.

Another thing Kami is thankful for is her mother taught her not to be judgmental and to be appreciative of what she had.

Also, Kami said her mother is a great 'nana'.

According to Kami, now that she and her siblings are older, her mother has become a really good mother to them. "She's there for everything and when I need her!"

Kami likes how her mother can be a 'goof ball'. She also praises her mother for completing her education. "Despite what she's been through." How ever, Kami found it difficult to talk to her about certain things, due to her mother being such a worrier. Kami worries that her mother won't try to get healthier mindset and not be such a worrier.

Kami has two daughters and described the relationship with her older daughter as 'rusty moments'. She finds herself yelling and her daughter becomes annoyed. Most of the time they are able to be close enough for her daughter and she to talk about anything and have fun. The younger daughter and Kami get along like 'little besties'.

Kyleigh

Kyleigh is the oldest of two sib-lings. She describes growing up in a normal and loving home.

Kyleigh said her mother is strict but loving. They got along well. Holidays are fun and they get together for meals and socializing with each other family members.

Kyleigh is thankful for her mother being supportive and encouraging education, and being so lovable and caring.

Kyleigh added, "She's almost always grumpy!"

The mother-daughter relationship remains good.

Lupe

Lupe is the second of eight sib-lings. She said she had a good childhood, but her mother was very strict. Holidays were fun and she and her family would get together r and prepare food and spend fun time with family.

Lupe's mother taught her how to cook and she said she is a good cook like her mother! The family and Lupe were close to their mother. The mother became sick and was strong and continued to be a mom and wife. Lupe described her after she was grown. Her mother and she became closer and would do fun things together.

Lupe thanks her mother for showing her how to be strong. Lupe has two daughters and she has taught them to be strong, to make sure their children come first, to stay close and to give thanks to the Lord for everything they have. The daughters and Lupe remain close and are grateful for having a strong mother and grandmother.

Ann Marie

Ann Marie is fifth of five siblings. According to Ann, the family didn't have much money but the parents made sure they were loved.

Ann added, "Our mom was selfless, she always put us before her and went without for us!" Ann said her mother taught them to treat others like they wanted to be treated, rich or poor. Ann remembered how her mother never took time for herself. Ann has two daughters and said they bump heads. She said she told her daughters she was their friend, but a mother first. The daughters didn't understand fully.,

Ann taught her daughters how to love one another be-cause after she's gone, all they will have been each other. Her daughters are mothers now and Ann gave them the advice to not follow her footsteps as she informed, she had made some bad choices in her life. Ac-cording to Ann, these choices affected her daughters.

Ann also advised her daughters to be the best moms possible, especially during their early years as they are the most impressionable and important years ever!

Amelia

Amelia is the youngest of six siblings. She remembers her growing up years as 'full of laughter'. Like most families, Amelia said they had disagreements but worked them out.

Amelia described her mother as a beautiful, strong woman. Her mom was single and worked hard to provide for them.

Amelia praised her mother for never 'giving up on us!' Amelia said her mom was too strict, but knew she had raised responsible daughters.

Holidays were fun and laughter with the family. Amelia said some sad times in her life were when her brother passed away and when her mother passed at age 84. Amelia has one daughter that she proudly raised with the same values her mother taught her.

Donna

Donna is the youngest of seven siblings. She described her life as being 'chaotic at times, but ideal and wonderful in many ways.' Donna said her birth mother became very ill with a brain tumor when Donna was three, had brain surgery which forced her to place Donna and her brother in foster care.

Donna recalled she had three foster moms and 'by and large got along with them'. She de-scribed her teen years as 'being stubborn and emotionally damaged'. Donna described each foster home as being different and that during her early life, her memories were very happy. Donna stated there were lots of happy laughter, cousins, food and some gifts. What Donna loved best about her biological mother loved her unconditionally, and Donna in-formed she 'never doubted that for a moment'.

Her primary foster mom was a WAC, ran a ranch with the assistance of twelve kids, and had been a teacher. Donna de-scribed her as being very wise, kind, loving and very strict.

Donna expressed how much she misses her as well as her birth mother very much.

She informed she had a foster mom in LA briefly and Donna stated, 'She would remind you of Jessica Rab-bitt, voluptuous, red-headed woman, married to a Cuban immigrant and she could sing like a movie star, there was always music in the house!'.

Donna stated that during her teen years her last foster mom was easy to talk to and was their church pianist and 'loved the Lord'. Donna regrets that her birth mom was unable to care for her and her brother following her surgery and said it was not her mom's fault. Donna recalled how her first foster mom could be judgmental, but a lovely woman otherwise.

She described foster mom number two, as being argumentative with her spouse. Donna stated, 'I just imagine they a very passionate love!'.

Foster mom number 3 was very cold at times, protecting her own feelings probably, Donna said. She did teach Donna how to sew. She is grateful that her birth mother taught her that love is the best thing you can give your child and that Jesus loved her.

Donna stated foster mom #one, taught her how to utilize banks, how to attain and maintain credit for her benefit. Mom number one taught her to be frugal, to give to the earth and reap the bounty, Livestock management, the reward of giving to others, and the value of education and learning.

Foster mom #2 taught Donna how amazing the Platters were. Donna said she was in love with Jimmy Hendrix at the time!

Donna concluded with 'God gave me four handsome sons and finally, one precious baby girl. We do get along, but the teen years were hard. She went against everything I had tried to teacher her. Now that she has children, she understands better! Donna believes in faith, family, country and the Golden Rule. Donna added, 'Maybe I am a better boy mom, because beauty and fashion have never been my strong suit'.

Carina

Carina was the youngest of five children. Three brothers and two sisters. According to Carina, her childhood was very happy ad she was to her mother, father and siblings. Carina and her siblings were born and raised in Mexico.

Holidays were happy times filled with joy and family gatherings at her parents' home.

Carina described her mother as being a fantastic cook and said for holidays and special occasions, her mother prepared Mexican meals of asado, tortillas, beans, (frijoles and charro), menudo and other delicious meals and pastries. With Carina being the youngest, she spent more time at while growing up. Her sib-lings were older and living their own lives.

Carina said although she was close to her parents, they did not verbally or physically ex-press affection. She stated that her grandmother lived an un-happy life with her grandfather and her mother had followed in her grandmother's footsteps.

Carina described her mother as being submissive to her husband, often times neglecting her own 'wants and needs'. Carina said her father was a good man to everyone but her mother. "My father was a good provider, willing to help any-one in need, and was a loving father to her, but not to her mother".

Carina said it was just under-stood that they (siblings) were loved although it was not ex-pressed. She describes how she is like their parents now.

Carina laughed and said she must have been her parents'
guardian in another life and her parents lovingly agreed.

Makayla

"I am the youngest of two sib-lings," said Makayla. "I would describe my relationship with my mother like a 'roller coaster ride."

Holidays were great when Makayla was a child. Her great-grandmother and grand-mother cooked delicious meals, tamales for Christmas, turkey and dressing for Thanksgiving and Easter. Christmas was Makayla's favorite time as the family would all congregate at her great-grandmother's and grandma's later on, and after her great-grandmother passed away. Makayla's grandma took over and planned all the holidays.

She liked the fact that her mother defended her and protected her whether Makayla was right or wrong. "I don't like the person she's turned into today!" Makayla explained that her mother's life style is questionable and inappropriate.

According to Makayla, she learned not to ever be like her mother. Makayla stated she hopes to be a good and loving grandmother some day!

She said she has a beautiful five-year-old daughter who is just like her! Makayla added that she will teach her daughter and son, to love, to be brave, and to believe that anything they set their mind to do, can be done! Makayla makes sure her children know that 'Mama will always be there!'

Oprah

Oprah was born to a single mother in Mississippi. She lived with her maternal grand-mother who physically abused her. Oprah later went to live with her mother Muturaukee where she was sexually abused by relatives and friends of the family (from the ages of 9-13). There was no daughter-mother bond.

Oprah ran away to live with her father and excelled in school and was off to her successful career.

Oprah opened up a Leader-ship Academy for Girls in South Africa in 2007. She mentors the young women and informed the first students are attending college in the US and still call on Oprah for advice and guidance. She has become a mom to these young ladies.

(As per Best of Personality Parade)

The Queen of TV rose from humble roots to become an entertainment mogul, and one of the world's most successful and inspiring women.

When Oprah became famous, her mother came around. Her mother became ill, and Oprah confronted her mother expressing everything she had been wanting to convey to her.

Oprah decided to forgive her mother, played music, and thanked her mother for having done the best she could.

Oprah stated that forgiveness, letting go and not holding grudges heals your pain and brings you peace.

-by Alison Ashton, *Personality Parade, 2018*

You are here not to shrink down to less, but to blossom into more of who you really are.

-Oprah Winfrey

Robin Roberts

According to Rocking Robin Production, Robin was raised in Mississippi on the gulf coast.

Her mother was Luci Marian Roberts and she was a social worker, educator, and chairperson of the Mississippi Board of Education.

Robin's father, Lawrence Roberts, was a Colonel in the US Air Force. Robin quoted her parents 'set the bar very high'. They made a lasting impact on her. Before Robin went on the air, she would blow two kisses, one for her mother and one for her father.

Robin was talented and ambitious and excelled in journalism. academically and in basketball. She began her journey in journalism. Robin joined Diane Sawyer and Charlie Gibson as co-anchor of Good Morning America. Her mother had a saying, 'Everybody's got something'. (according to a book with Veronica Chambers) her how to treasure.

Robin states her mother taught her how to treasure moments from her world travels, hugs, aromas of food, devotion and faith. Robin explained how her mother bought herself a baby grand piano and told her family she was going to place a sign in the yard that said, 'I'm spending by children's inheritance.' The mother also wanted a stone fireplace, had It built, and never used it!

Robin had been feeling ill herself was diagnosed with breast cancer and a fatal blood disease. She survived both. Her mother visited Robin during her breast cancer treatment.

Robin's mother began to get sick and passed away. Robin kissed her mom's face and held her hand until she passed away.

Joann

Joann was the first of four siblings. She was raised by her parents in a home filled with 'Lots of love'. Joann said she got along well with her mom and still do! Except her mom calls her Joanna and Joann said, "My name is Joann!"

Joann described her mom as a stay-at-home mom, and her mom teaching them how to cook, clean and iron. According to Joann, she is thankful to her mother for having taught them how to be respectful and to treat others good.

Joann also is grateful for her mother 'always being there for us, in case we needed anything'.

Holidays were fun filled with laughter, family, and lots of delicious food prepared and gifts for holidays and birthdays.

Joann has one daughter, and she has taught her to be independent, to treat people the way she wants to be treated, and to work hard so she will never do without, and to treat her husband and daughters with respect.

Joann continues to be close with her mother and siblings.

"This is My Daughter, Ruby"

Jamie Lee Curtis' daughter Ruby, then 'Tom', had been attempting to come out as a Trans and talk to her parents about her decision. She was unable to voice it to her parents so she sent her mother a text and her mother immediately and Jamie said there were tears involved.

Ruby had come out to her friend, now wife, about being different. According to Jamie it was difficult to get used to calling her trans daughter Ruby. They had been so used to calling out the other name, 'Tom'.

Jamie said she and her husband still slip up. Daughter Ruby stated it's okay with her.

It appears that Jamie learned a lot from Ruby, and they remain close. Jamie is supportive of Ruby and they have a daughter-mother relationship.

Ruby did go to therapy, still being 'Tom' but described having a 'bad experience'.

-Jason Sheeler, People Maga-

zine, November 2021

Iylana

Fix Our Lives - Oprah Winfrey Network

In this particular episode, Iyanla is visiting a mother and daughter who are screaming at the top of their lungs at each other.

I felt sorry for Iyanla at first because she was unable to get a word in edgewise! She soon was able to calm the two down, somewhat.

The daughter informed Iyanla that the mother was just plain mean, and was jealous of her. The mama had been a nurse but had lost her license due to taking her patients' medications.

She attempted suicide. The daughter stated her mother didn't want to die, just wanted attention. The mother didn't agree with the daughter's life. The mother admitted that she also gambled away the children's money, drank, and had received a few DWI's. She also admitted to have failed her children. The daughter was surprised and saddened by the mother's disclosure about cutting her wrists, and learning that her mother had been physically abused in her past.

Iyanla was able to get the mother and daughter to listen to one another and to begin to form a mother-daughter relationship, hopefully.

Do the best you can until you know better. Then, when you know better, do better.

- Maya Angelou

I hope that when you look in the mirror, you see the awesomeness of God's divine creation staring back at you.

- Brave Girl

Don't forget to open the blinds every morning and let the sunshine and blessings of each day come in!

-Viola Arriola